To David,
This book
is a lot better
than The Rest of. "

Stan Levco
1/29/15

The Second Best of Stan Levco

STAN LEVCO

ISBN: 978-1-4834-1501-7 (sc)
ISBN: 978-1-4834-1500-0 (e)

Library of Congress Control Number: 2014912673

Because of the dynamic nature of the Internet, any web addresses or links contained in
this book may have changed since publication and may no longer be valid. The views
expressed in this work are solely those of the author and do not necessarily reflect the
views of the publisher, and the publisher hereby disclaims any responsibility for them.

Any people depicted in stock imagery provided by Thinkstock are models,
and such images are being used for illustrative purposes only.
Certain stock imagery © Thinkstock.

Lulu Publishing Services rev. date: 08/14/2014

Contents

Chapter 3: Shoe in middle of road is a foot over my head

Chapter 4: Running for office from 20 points behind

Chapter 5: Actor did it his way – in a gorilla costume

Chapter 6: Man of the year certainly big enough to wear crown

Chapter 7: From a world far, far away (my world)

About the Author

Stan Levco practices law as a part-time deputy prosecutor in Tell City, Indiana, and he works as a special prosecutor throughout the state of Indiana. Levco lives in Evansville, Indiana, with his wife Susie. He is the father of two daughters. This is his second book.

Foreword

Stan Levco inspired me to write silly stuff—and still does.

When I was a teen, I looked forward to his columns in the Evansville newspaper. The regional paper, with a decent-sized circulation, was my window to the world.

Many times, after I parted the curtains for a view of the world, I would find Stan peering in at me with that crazed look of his. It was creepy. We called the cops. Stan was never caught, though we did find a Boston Red Sox cap in a shrub just outside the window.

Stan, via his column, introduced me to satire. An online dictionary defines satire as "the use of irony, sarcasm, ridicule, or the like, in exposing, denouncing, or deriding vice, folly, etc."

In layman's terms, satire is "a license to be a smartass."

When I was a kid, dad always told me to "stop being a smartass," yet Stan, an adult (based on appearance), demonstrated it was OK to be one—a successful one to boot!

Stan's satirical column always made me laugh. More importantly, it made me want to write a column of my own. I'm willing to bet that I'm not the only person Stan has inspired to write—in those other cases though it has likely been "hate" mail, not a column. It happens. Trust me.

Fast forward to 2011 or so. I finally met up with Stan (at least I think it was him) at a coffee shop. He agreed to meet after learning he had influenced me to be humor columnist. We talked. We laughed. I bought his lunch.

He told me he was trying to decide whether or not to begin writing a column again now that he was no longer Evansville's prosecuting attorney, a position he'd held from 1991 to 2010.

You should, I told him.

He said something like, "Well...I don't know. Maybe I have already written all there is for me to write."

Bull..., I thought.

"Do it," I said.

Ultimately, he did it.

And he is still doing it—much to my joy and amusement—and he's doing it quite well.

Clearly, his ink well has not gone dry.

Best of all, his writing has become better with age.

Stan losing his last election was the best thing to happen to the Tri-State—we got his column back. Not to mention this second collection of columns. The verdict is in: this is a funny, funny book— and you are better off (and so is Stan) for having bought it.

This new collection verifies that Stan is still a wonderful smartass—albeit, an older, wiser one.

It also verifies that I still want to be like Stan when I don't grow up.

--Scott Saalman, Humor Columnist, The Herald
(Jasper, Indiana); author, Nose Hairs Gone Wild;
founder, Will Read and Sing For Food.

Preface

My first book, *The Best of Stan Levco*, was published in 1986. At the time, I'd hoped it would be the first of many.

But *The Best of Stan Levco*, whatever artistic success it may have achieved, was something other than a spectacular financial success. And having stopped writing after getting elected Prosecutor meant no new material. So my plans for the sequel had to be put on the shelf.

But over the years, I've never been able to let go of the thought of seeing more of my columns in book form. Once I began writing again regularly in 2012, a sequel to *The Best of Stan Levco* became inevitable.

Why did I want this book published?

Was it because of a demanding public? Not exactly. While people occasionally tell me they like my columns, I can't recall anyone suggesting that I compile them in book form.

A desire to make money, perhaps? Not really. I wouldn't mind making a profit, but I'll be overjoyed to break even.

Was it to share my ideas with the world? Perhaps in a small part. I take a great deal of pleasure when I discover someone likes something I wrote. And publishing a book gives me the chance to have more people read more of my columns, which is a good transition for the bottom line reason I wanted to have this book published.

Ego.
Pure unadulterated ego.

Look what I wrote. Isn't it clever? Look at me. I wrote a book.

I am dedicating this book to my two daughters in chronological order – Jessica and Jeanine. It has crossed my mind on more than one occasion that I'd like them to have this tangible object to remember me by.

A project like this doesn't happen overnight and without the help of many people. I couldn't print these columns without the permission of the *Evansville Courier and Press*, *The Prosecutor*, and *Evansville Living*.

"Teaching the truth about justice," "Not ready for prime time," "Running for office from 20 points behind," "A prosecuting attorney is exactly who I am," "A fair and impartial juror," and "Prosecuting kiosks can be hazardous to your health" are reprinted in this book by permission of *The Prosecutor*, Rhapsody in Blue is reprinted by permission of *Evansville Living*, and all others are reprinted by permission of the *Evansville Courier and Press*.

Dale McConnaghay gave me the opportunity to begin writing for the *Evansville Press* in the early 1980's and Linda Negro gave me a second chance to write some of my second best columns.

Joe Rhodes shot the book cover and illustrated some of the columns.

Bob Pigman, Rick Young, and Erin Bauer were kind enough to help me choose which columns to include and Amanda Pharr, Barber & Bauer, LLP, had the arduous task, along with Lulu Publishing, of putting it all together.

I hope you, the reader, enjoy the book.

And I hope I break even.

CHAPTER

1

Old self waited near jukebox

Old self waited near jukebox

I've been going to Bloomington, -Ind., a lot lately to work on a case. It's been over 15 years since I graduated from law school there and until recently I hadn't been there much since graduation.

Getting back near campus has made me nostalgic for those college days, so for the past few weeks I'd been searching unsuccessfully for my old self.

This week, on a hunch, I stopped by the Memorial Union and there he was, my old self, sitting at a table near the jukebox.

"Mind if I sit down?" I asked.

He motioned to the empty chair.

I started to introduce myself. "You're not going to believe this, but I'm…"

"I know who you are. I've been expecting you."

"How did you know I'd be back?"

"Everyone comes back looking for who he used to be. Some people just take longer than others."

"I've been looking everywhere for you," I said.

"Really? Where?"

"The motels where I've stayed, the courthouse, restaurants. I couldn't find anyone who knew where I could find you."

"Of course not," he said. "We're two totally different people now. We may be staying in the same town, but you never go to the places I go to anymore. Do you think I'd ever go to a restaurant that costs more than $3 for dinner?"

"I guess you're right, but we've still got a lot in common."

"Like what?"

"I still look a lot like you."

"Not really. How old are you anyway?"

"Forty, but I don't feel any different."

"Well, you look old enough to be my father."

"Hey, I didn't come here to be insulted. If you want me to leave, just say so."

"I was just kidding. There's still a resemblance. I don't mind if you stay. I'm just killing time anyway."

"Shouldn't you be studying?"

"Give me a break. I thought you of all people would understand. My courses are irrelevant. Like, who cares about corporations?"

"Don't knock it. There's a lot of money to be made in corporate law."

"So what? When I get out of here I'm going to defend poor people unjustly accused of crimes."

"You'd be surprised. Things change. Your perspective changes."

"I suppose you looked me up to impart some great pearls of wisdom. Am I right, mister?"

"No. And even if I did, you wouldn't listen."

"Probably not, but try me."

"OK. Just enjoy what you're doing now."

"I am."

"No. I mean really enjoy it. Savor it. Don't waste so much time. Once you leave here, you'll never be able to get it back."

"Is it that bad out there?"

"No, it's not that bad. Just different. Look kid, this isn't what I thought it was going to be. I've got to go back to my motel room."

"Mister, before you go. You must know everything that happens – if I graduated, what happened in Vietnam, if I got married, what kind of president Nixon turned out to be. Right?"

"Right. What do you want to know?"

"Did the Red Sox ever win the World Series?"

Learning to play "Rhapsody in Blue"-one note at a time

Last spring I took my eldest daughter Jessica to Chicago to interview for an internship. The night before, we attended a play about the life of George Gershwin. On the drive back, I told Jessica I'd once seriously considered hiring a piano teacher to teach me to play Gershwin's "Rhapsody in Blue?"

"But you don't know how to play the piano," she said.

"A minor obstacle," I responded. "My theory was this: I could easily learn the first note. Right?"

I had her there.

"If I could learn the first note, then I could learn the second, then the third," I continued. "There are a finite number of notes in the piece. Way fewer than grains of sand on the beach. Eventually, I could learn the whole thing!"

"Then why don't you still do it?" She asked.

She had me there.

When I got back to Evansville I approached Janet Voyles, my youngest daughter Jeanine's music teacher. I explained my theory to her. "I don't want to learn how to read music — or play the scales — or do anything else," I said. "It's either the Rhapsody one note at a time — or nothing."

Voyles, who's taught many students over the years many different instruments, but none under the One Note at a Time Theory, was skeptical, but agreeable. "If you're willing to try to learn it that way," she said, "I'm willing to try to teach you." And so, in May 2005, it came to pass: I began trying to learn "Rhapsody in Blue" — one note at a time.

At first it was painful to the ear. And at second, it was painful to the ear. The version Voyles selected had eight pages, about forty stanzas, and more than one thousand notes. My weekly lessons consisted of her playing a few stanzas, and then numbering the notes for me according to a numbering system I invented. Then I practiced those stanzas for a week, and then moved onto the next week — one note at a time.

Although I saw chronological progress, I began to question whether I'd ever play it decently for others. I was optimistic I could get through it, which was my minimal goal, but it wasn't sounding anything like Mr. Gershwin intended. My hope was once I completed it, I could begin polishing my very rough version — one page at a time. Still, by late November, I thought with another month's practice, I could bring closure to my noble experiment and the first day of the new year seemed like the obvious time for my debut.

Originally, I thought I'd premiere the piece at our house. But after realizing our family room was too small — and more importantly, not majestic enough for the occasion — I started searching for other venues. Soon, it became clear that no place other than The Victory Theatre in Downtown Evansville would do.

For the month of December, I became a practicing Rhapsody-in-Blue-fiend. As the days progressed more rapidly than my improvement, I began to get increasingly concerned that I was going to make a big Rhapsody-in-Blue-fool of myself. For the three days before the big event, I didn't get a single decent night's sleep. One night I dreamed I arrived late for the performance and when I sat down to the piano, instead of 88 symmetrical keys, I was greeted by a semicircle of rotten teeth in various shapes and shades.

I awoke on the first day of the new year, counting the hours to my 5 p.m. appointment with destiny. As planned, I arrived at the Victory early to practice, then to hide so I could make a dramatic entrance, clad in my borrowed blue sequined jacket.

I knew I'd be nervous, but with a half-hour to go, panic set in. I couldn't remember the beginning. I was by myself trying to pantomime the notes — and I'd forgotten how to start. Then I realized my fingers were sweating. Brow sweat wouldn't have surprised me, or even sweat under my arms. But finger sweat?

As soon as I was introduced, I knew I was in trouble. When I sat down at the piano, it was worse than I imagined. My sweaty fingers were now shaking. Somehow I got through the beginning without a major mistake. The shaking subsided some, and realizing I might get through it, I gained a little confidence. It wasn't pretty, but I did it. After eight months, more than 30 lessons and well over 100 hours of practice, I played the entire "Rhapsody in Blue" — one note at a time.

The next day — before I really had time to bask in the glow of my achievement — Jessica called to make sure I didn't get complacent.

"Well, Dad, that was good, but it's time to move on. You need to do something else this year," she said.

I thought for a moment: "I used to write a little," I said. "Maybe I'll see if I can get something published in a magazine."

Kokomo overrun by AIPS; spread feared

An outbreak of an insidious disease is spreading through Kokomo, Ind. at an alarming rate. The disease is called Addictive Ideological Psychosis Syndrome, or AIPS, for short.

AIPS has been around since the beginning of time but has mutated into many different forms. Unlike victims of AIDS who suffer from a degeneration of blood cells, AIPS victims suffer from poisoned cells of vital organs, including the brain and heart.

Although both sexes and all ages, except the very young, are susceptible, most of those diagnosed as having the disease in Kokomo are parents of middle school children.

The presence of AIPS in Kokomo has been suspected by the medical community for months, but scientists did not confirm the diagnosis until last weekend when hundreds of residents packed a local gymnasium to raise money to prevent AIDS victim Ryan White from returning to school.

One scientist admitted that despite the obvious other signs of the disease, it was the cheering mob in the gymnasium who raised $12,000 to keep the 14-year-old boy out of school that forced him to confirm his diagnosis.

While some physical effects of the disease vary with the individual, almost all victims suffer from a weak heart and some doctors claim to have treated victims with ice water in their veins.

No one knows for certain where the disease began. Some scientists believe it originated with South African barracudas.

The jury is still out as to whether or not the disease is contagious. However, scientists are alarmed at the rapid increase in reported cases. What was just a handful of a suspected cases a year ago has now increased to thousands. Some scientists speculate the disease can be transmitted orally–through word of mouth.

Also, although there is no medical proof to support this theory, doctors have discovered that simply being in a crowd of AIPS sometimes turns previously rational people into part of the afflicted. Until more research has been completed, health authorities are strongly advising limited contact with AIPS victims.

Sadly, there is still no cure for the disease, although it often goes into remission if the object of the sufferer's psychosis is removed. In that case, many victims have been known to lead essentially normal lives until another cause crops up and the cycle begins again.

One of the most frightening aspects of the problem is that scientists believe we all have the virus in our systems, but there's really no way to tell from individual to individual just how much peer pressure and fear it takes to activate the disease.

Catfish heaven sounds kinda fishy

There's this woman, kind of sexy yet innocent at the same time. She's smiling at me from my TV and telling me in a sweet Southern accent that Long John Silver's wants to take my mouth to catfish heaven.

Before the ad, I didn't even know there was a catfish heaven. But I wonder why they want to take my mouth there, or, more importantly, why they think my mouth would want to go there.

I assume catfish would be interested in going to catfish heaven. Shouldn't the advertising be directed at catfish? I'd think a human body part would be hopelessly out of place.

Where is catfish heaven, anyway? I always thought there was just one great big heaven, but I guess heaven's compartmentalized. Perhaps catfish heaven is right around the bend from Cajun shrimp heaven and red snapper heaven.

It stands to reason if there's a catfish heaven, there must be a catfish hell. It's really hard to imagine what terrible misdeed would warrant a catfish being relegated to catfish hell. I just know my mouth has no interest in going there.

If I let them take my mouth to catfish heaven, I wonder what it would do when it arrived. Would there be other human mouths it could talk to? Maybe it would be surrounded by angelic catfish with halos. I wouldn't think a dead catfish could carry on a very interesting conversation with my mouth and I doubt if my mouth would be interested in trying to eat a catfish in heavenly form, particularly in its own heaven.

I'm also worried about whether we're talking about a one-way or a round trip. What if my mouth decides to go and there's no way back.

Another thing that perplexes me is what's the rest of my body supposed to do when my mouth is living it up in catfish heaven. I think I'd be more inclined to encourage the journey if some of the rest of me were allowed to make stops at other heavens. I'm sure my ears would love to spend a few days in rock 'n' roll heaven.

I'll admit I'm tempted to accept the offer. But until I get some answers to my questions, I think my mouth will be staying right here on earth.

Prince may need job till king's ransom paid

Prince Charles is facing a mid-life crisis. His young wife is enjoying the Britain night life without him. And his mother shows no signs of giving up her throne, voluntarily or otherwise, to her heir.

This leaves Charles drifting in regal limbo. This situation prompted Labor Party leader Neil Kinnock to suggest that Charles be given an "important public position," a sentiment I'm sure Joe Biden would echo.

But what if Parliament doesn't give the prince an important position? Maybe he'd have to apply for a job, like the rest of us.

***

"I've read your resume and I'm very impressed with your educational background, but I noticed you left 'previous experience' blank. Do you have any previous experience, Chuck?"

"If you don't mind terribly, I'd rather you call me Charles."

"OK, Charles. Do you have any previous experience, Charles?"

"Not really. I've been prince ever since I can remember."

"You mean 'Purple Rain'? That Prince?"

"No, I'm the Prince of Wales."

"Sure you are and I'm the Duke of Earl. I suppose your wife is a princess, too."

"As a matter of fact, yes."

"OK, why not? Do you have any particular salary requirements, Prince?"

"I've been receiving an allowance of over $2 million a year plus free food and lodging and unlimited use of a polo field in summer. I suppose something along those lines would do nicely."

"Would that figure be negotiable?"

"I'd give it a go, if the right position came along."

"Just what kind of job skills do you have?"

"Oh, you know, wear uniforms, visit places, present myself, ride in carriages. Things like that."

"Well, Prince, I'm afraid we don't have much demand for carriage riders. Exactly what kind of position were you looking for?"

"Actually, I'd like to be King. If it wouldn't be too much trouble."

"King of what?"

"Of a country. It doesn't have to be England. Any small monarchy would do for starters."

"How about a knight? I might have an opening for a knight in shining armor."

"What's it pay?"

"I'm afraid the starting pay would be low, but there's plenty of room for advancement and the fringes are unbelievable. You'll find an unlimited number of damsels in distress, and what you do with them, well, that's between you and the damsels. Know what I mean?"

"I think so."

"Say, can you ride a white horse, Prince?"

"Sure, but I don't think I want to be a knight. I really kind of have my heart set on being King."

"All right, I get the picture. But we just don't have anything in the way of King right now. Tell you what. I'll keep your resume on file and as soon as something comes up, I'll give you a call."

Whoa, Katie! Give an old guy a break

Larry King takes Katie Couric out on a date and then after dinner tries to seduce her at his apartment.

Sounds like a premise for a bad Super Bowl commercial, but according to Katie, that's exactly what happened about 20 years ago.

In an interview with Jimmy Kimmel last week, Katie revealed that she accepted a date with the former CNN talk show host, explaining at the time she would go out with anyone who asked, because "you learn something anytime you're with someone new."

When Larry made his move, Kate politely demurred, saying she'd prefer someone her own age. That politeness disappeared last week when she couldn't resist the urge to tell Jimmy and a national TV audience about old Larry's feeble incomplete pass.

Her calling him out would have been justified if Larry had hurt, frightened or even offended her, but Katie wasn't recounting a night of terror. She was "humorously" sharing with anyone who would listen how pathetic Larry was on this date.

She sarcastically referred to his healthy dinner choice of poached veal in chicken stock, necessitated by his recent quadruple bypass surgery, as "hot." Making fun of someone's dinner order, particularly if it's for health reasons, is hitting below the suspenders, in my book.

And then she made light of the numerous keys to the city that Larry had displayed in his apartment. Can't a guy take pride in his awards without being ridiculed?

I'm not convinced the age disparity was the only reason Katie shot him down. In her defense, the thought of Larry trying to make that kind of connection has a certain creepy quality, reminiscent of last week's Super Bowl commercial with the sexy model kissing the geek. The problem with the twosome in the ad had nothing to do with age. And with all due respect to Larry's seven wives, if I were casting the role of male sex symbol, Larry would not be near the top of the list, even in his prime.

But whatever the reason, was it really necessary for Katie to blab about it on national TV? She's the one who got Larry's hopes up by accepting the date. And while that doesn't entitle him to much, I think he should at least be entitled to a modicum of discretion. Apparently, discretion was not one of the new things she learned on her dates.

And it's not just the fact she felt compelled to share the details of the evening that bothers me. Her timing and the present status of her victim compound the transgression.

Katie's interview with Sarah Palin about four years ago did as much as anything to help prevent the Alaskan Governor from becoming Vice President. Sarah and her supporters could legitimately claim how destructive the interview was, but at least Katie was picking on someone who had the means to fight back. And stopping Sarah Palin from getting elected would arguably be a beneficial goal. What possible good can come from trashing Larry?

And why now? Perhaps if she spoke out 10 years ago, Larry would have at least had the opportunity to defend himself on his talk show. But now Larry's relegated to a web show. He's had multiple heart surgeries and although all of us have limited time left, you get the feeling Larry's time is more limited than most. Shouldn't he have been permitted to spend that time basking in the glow of his role as American icon?

But no. Larry now has to spend his remaining days humiliated by Katie's public trashing. What's next for Katie?

Shooting fish in a barrel?

'Disease' could make
many lives miserable

As if I didn't have enough to worry about, now I discover that Boston Red Sox batting champ Wade Boggs has suffered for four years from the disease of being oversexed.

Boggs, who is involved in a $12 million lawsuit with his ex-paramour, Margo Adams, said in a recent "Geraldo" show about oversexed people made him realize he had the disease.

The newspaper article said that Boggs "suffered from the disease." I'm embarrassed to admit my ignorance, but before I read the article, I didn't know an oversexed person had a disease or that there was much suffering involved. But apparently it's so.

Boggs said, "It's a sad thing to say, but it engulfed me and the situation kept getting worse."

Sometimes appearances are deceiving. Here's Boggs, young, handsome, making over a million dollars a year for playing baseball, and all the time he's in the clutches of this horrible disease. I had no idea.

If it could happen to Boggs, there's no telling how many others out there in the general population are similarly afflicted.

Just this week it was revealed that Secretary of Defense-designate John Tower's nomination is in trouble because Tower had reportedly been drinking in bars in the company of women. And while the reports made no mention of his suffering, one can only assume he hated every minute of it.

Now that Boggs has courageously brought this problem out in the open, we obviously need to do something about it. What I suggest is we launch an all-out war against the oversexed and stop this disease before it reaches epidemic proportions. If we can appoint Bill Bennett to the position of drug czar, surely there's room in the Cabinet for an oversexed czar.

But I'm concerned that with a budget that can't properly fund AIDS research or the war on drugs, needed treatment for the oversexed will be placed on the back burner.

It may seem like a small problem now, but I'd venture to guess that if left untreated, within five years everyone will have a friend or a relative who's oversexed. It's not a pretty picture.

We need money for research because there's so little we know about the disease. Is it contagious? Is it curable? And if so, is abstinence the only cure?

Can someone be infected, yet lead a useful life? Does it afflict females as well as males? Are there any Oversexed Anonymous clubs? If so, where are they located?

If you help a person cover up for this disease, are you helping that person? Are there people who are carriers, but don't exhibit symptoms?

If we don't answer these questions soon, it may soon be too late.

Think hard, Cubs fans:
Is big win really worth it?

Dear Chicago Cubs fans:

So the Chicago Cubs have won their division and you think they're going to beat San Francisco for their first pennant since 1945. You could be right.

And then you have visions of them beating the American League champs to win the first World Series since Teddy Roosevelt was president. You might be right again.

You've suffered through the '50s and '60s when "Let's play two" generally meant they'd lose two that day instead of one. You agonized in 1969 when they blew a nine-game lead in the last month. Your heart was broken in 1984 when they lost three in a row to San Diego.

You've waited all your life for this moment and you think that a World Series at Wrigley would be fantastic.

Well, think again, Bunky, because if the Cubs win the World Series it could be the worst thing that could possibly happen to you.

I speak from experience. I've rooted for the Red Sox all my life and while that's not exactly the same as being a Cubs fan, it's pretty close.

I've survived them losing to the Cardinals in 1967. I endured as they were the losing team in the greatest World Series ever played in 1975. And I agonized when Bunky Dent hit that home run in 1978.

19

But a strange thing happened in 1986. It looked as if that would finally be the year my dream came true. The Red Sox were one pitch away from winning it all.

I remember watching the game on television, cheering in anticipation of finally seeing my Red Sox doused with World Series champagne.

But I started to wonder: What am I going to do now? Now that the Red Sox have finally won the big one, what's left to cheer for?

Fortunately, I was saved from the ultimate victory and I can still enjoy wondering whether this will actually be the year.

That's what it's all about. Pushing that boulder up the hill until you almost get to the top, having the boulder fall down and then pushing it back up again. The thrill is in the struggle, not in the accomplishment. If you reach your ultimate goal, there are no more goals left to live for.

The charm of the Cubs is they are losers. They never quite reach the top of the hill. If they didn't break your hearts, you wouldn't love them. If they become winners, they wouldn't be the Cubs anymore.

I'm not suggesting you should want them to lose against San Francisco. And it wouldn't be unwise to hope they win three World Series games.

But if you really root for them to win it all, be prepared to suffer the consequences the rest of your life.

Sincerely,
Someone who's been there.

That day in Dallas still fresh in memory

For my parents, it was December 7, 1941. For my kids, it will be September 11, 2001. For me, it's November 22, 1963.

Everyone of my generation remembers what they were doing when they heard the news. I was returning from my grandmother's funeral, stopped off at my uncle's house, and watched the news on a black and white TV.

It's not an exaggeration to say I felt far worse about Kennedy's death than my grandmother's, which is only partially attributable to the circumstances of their deaths. My feelings were hardly unique, but while many of us baby boomers felt a connection with Kennedy, I believe mine was stronger then most.

For starters, I lived in Brookline, Mass., less than a 10-minute walk from Kennedy's birthplace. I saw him briefly three times. The first time, I was only a few feet away when I ran after him as he rode in his open-air convertible on a football field in Portland, Maine, during his 1960 campaign for President. One of my friends excitedly bragged that he touched him.

I was working as a dishwasher at Children's Hospital in the summer of 1963, where his son Patrick died and I caught a glimpse of him as he walked down the hallway. And I attended a political fundraiser for him in Boston about a month before the assassination, tickets courtesy of the aforementioned uncle.

The assassination happened during my senior year of high school and it was not only depressing, but disorienting. It did not seem possible. I've never had that reaction to a disaster since.

My high school yearbook that spring recorded my life's ambition: To be the first lawyer to successfully defend Jack Ruby. This was my adolescent way of proclaiming my affection for President Kennedy. I'm not sure which of my philosophies has undergone a greater transformation since — that my goal was to be a defense attorney or that I thought taking the law into your own hands, like Ruby did, was acceptable, even praiseworthy behavior.

Back then, it was pretty much accepted that Lee Harvey Oswald acted alone. Since then, thanks to a society that is far more cynical about the government and almost everything else, about 75 percent of the American public thinks that Oswald was part of a conspiracy.

Count me in the remaining 25 percent. I not only think Oswald acted alone, I'm certain of it. We all have indicators that we believe reveal important information about others. I can't judge a person by their politics (although I can make an exception if their politics are really extreme) or favorite TV show, but someone's opinion on whether Lee Harvey Oswald acted alone is very revealing to me.

When I am a guest speaker on law, I routinely poll audiences on that question, but I have found the results frustrating and disappointing. Virtually every one of my informal polls has tallied a majority of conspiracy theorists, even among prosecutors.

I have no question that Oswald acted alone, yet how one disgruntled person can single-handedly and profoundly change the course of history has always been difficult to accept in a world that I like to believe is governed by some sense of rationality and fairness.

I wonder how my life and the history of the United States and the world would have been different, if only any number of factors had prevented those shots from reaching their target.

Stephen King's recent book, "11/22/63," has an interesting take on that question, essentially suggesting things would have been worse. There's obviously no way of knowing for sure, although it doesn't seem like a greater good would come from such a despicable act. However, the only certainty is things would have been different.

It doesn't seem possible it's been 50 years. The events of that Friday afternoon remain fresh in my memory. I've never stopped thinking about that day in Dallas.

Passing out is always consciousness-lowering

Some people pass footballs. Some pass kidney stones. Others pass "Go."

I pass out.

I did it again Dec. 17 after the 5-mile "Jingle Bell Run" in Darmstadt, Ind. My hands froze, and when I got inside the building with all the other finishers and my hands began to thaw, I crumpled.

It's not fun to pass out, but I've had a lot of practice at it.

About 20 years ago, I collapsed at the dining commons at the University of Massachusetts–before I ate the food. I might have forgotten about it if it hadn't made such an impression on the bystanders.

Apparently those who witnessed it will never forget it–or at least never let me forget it. This summer during my 20-year college reunion, two people said, "Hey, Levco, remember that time you fainted in the dining commons?"

Somehow, I'd hoped my four years in college would have produced memories among my peers more significant than my falling head first onto the floor. Oh to see ourselves as others see us.

The frequency of my passing out has decreased over the years. About 15 years ago, the week after my wedding, I was playing in a tennis tournament. The dozen or so spectators, including my new bride, were treated to watching me take a dive on the court. Unfortunately, I wasn't going after a ball at the time.

There was a lot of chuckling among those present about how the honeymoon weekend must have been responsible, which I readily agreed to once I regained consciousness. That seemed preferable to explaining that I just faint every now and then.

My honeymoon weekend swoon didn't have anything to do with cold hands since it happened in June. But, as I think back on it, I vaguely remember something about cold feet.

Since that honeymoon week, I've only passed out a few times, and, with the exception of the run, it's always been in the privacy of my home.

That's how I prefer it. I still haven't figured out a way to faint with grace and dignity, but at least when you're alone, you don't have people staring at you.

You can flop onto your bed. You can careen into walls, crawl to the bathroom and moan pitifully to your heart's content without worrying about drawing a crowd.

The last few times I've passed out, including last weekend, have all been the result of the same thing–cold hands. If I'm going to faint after a race in public, I'd like it to be for something a little more macho than cold hands.

I remember reading a couple of years ago that a guy actually got shot in the head during the Boston Marathon, but still finished the race.

As I was gracelessly and undignifiedly lying on the floor last Saturday while the crowd stared, I could hear voices in the background.

"What's the matter with him?"

"Cold hands."

"No, I mean, why did he pass out?"

"That's the reason. I heard him say his hands got cold."

"You've gotta be kidding."

As I was drifting in and out, I wanted to shout, "Hey, I took a bullet in my right temple, but nothing was going to stop me from finishing the race."

I even thought of saying, "I just got married last week and I guess my honeymoon just took too much out of me."

I probably would have said it if I thought anyone would have believed me.

Putting the Scrooges to holiday is a tradition

The world can be divided into two kinds of people: Christmas people and non-Christmas people. I'm in the latter category; Mrs. Levco is definitely in the former.

I was turned down for the part of Scrooge in my junior high school play, probably because it seemed too much like typecasting. Susie, on the other hand, counts among her favorite all-time albums, "Barbra Streisand, a Christmas Album" and "Elvis Sings the Wonderful World of Christmas."

The only real enjoyment I get out of the holiday season is complaining about it.

I like to begin my complaining around Thanksgiving–Can you believe how early they're getting the Christmas decorations out this year? – and continue through the weeks approaching Christmas Day – Should we really spend so much money on a tree? Why don't we just get a plastic one and get it over with?

I like to complain about the Christmas songs on the radio, the stories on TV, the number of people we're getting presents for and the amount we're spending. If I'm really on a roll, I might question the wisdom of including someone on our Christmas card list.

My better half seems totally oblivious to my attempts to crush the Christmas spirit. She bakes multicolored Christmas cookies, makes Christmas decorations for the tree, and strings the outside of our house with Christmas lights.

Given the difference in our philosophy, it's not surprising that she's the Levco in charge of buying Christmas presents, a task she approaches with a zeal not unlike Larry Bird preparing for a new basketball season.

As soon as one Christmas is over, she begins planning for the next one: You know, those glass bowls I saw at the flea market would be just perfect for Aunt Katherine for next Christmas.

During the year when we're with potential gift recipients, when Christmas is the last thing on my mind, she'll be looking for clues from a person's clothing or dishes or some offhand remark that will help her select just the right gift.

In September and October, she pores through ads and dozens of Christmas catalogs and goes to store, reviewing the merchandise and prices, so that by November she can concentrate on the few remaining who still do not have the perfect gift. By December, whenever everyone else is making last minute selections, she's wrapping.

In less than a week, another Christmas will be history. I'll have to wait about 11 months before I can complain again. For Susie, it'll be business as usual.

As far as winning goes, it's thought that counts

Tuesday's election will produce countless winners and acceptance speeches. When you listen to the speeches this time, try to imagine what the winner is really thinking.

***

Gosh, I don't know what to say. (*So I suppose I'll just give the acceptance speech I've been practicing for three weeks.*) First, I'd like to thank my wife, without whose constant encouragement this great victory wouldn't have been possible. (*Unless you count the dozens of times she threatened to divorce me if I ran for public office.*)

Tonight's victory is not a victory of party. (*No, it's a victory for me personally.*) Nor is it a victory for me personally. (*I wonder what it would be like to live in the White House?*) But rather it represents a victory for the people. (*Particularly the people who contributed to my campaign.*)

When I ran for this office, I promised to help the little man. (*If you're a jockey, you've struck pay–dirt. For the rest of you, it'll be more of the same.*) And that's a promise I intend to keep. (*There's a first time for everything.*)

I wish to extend my heartfelt congratulations to my opponent. (*Better luck next time, Bozo.*) He ran an aggressive campaign. (*He fought dirty.*) And he has nothing to be ashamed of. (*Other than the fact the voters overwhelmingly rejected him.*)

I look forward to the challenges ahead. (*If I can just stay away from controversy, they'll never get me out of here.*)

I wish I could thank each of you personally. (*But since each of you would probably ask me for a favor, I won't.*) But time doesn't permit me to do that. (*Although I did have enough time to ask each of you personally for a cash contribution.*)

My door will always be open. (*How often I'll be behind it is another question.*) And don't ever worry about calling me at home. (*If you can find my unlisted home phone number.*)

Thank you and God bless you. (*Thank God I won't have to go through this ordeal for another four years.*)

CHAPTER

2

Scissors remain through thick, thin

Scissors remain
through thick, thin

I have these scissors.

You can't tell they're special just by looking at them, but what's unusual is my relationship with these scissors. And any time you use the word "relationship" describing your scissors, it's a pretty good bet there is going to be something unusual. In this case, what distinguishes these scissors from ordinary scissors is how long the two (three, if you think of scissors as a pair) of us have been together.

Some people can remember the moment they first saw their spouse. While my relationship with my scissors has lasted longer than most marriages, I can't pinpoint the precise moment, although I can narrow it down to sometime in September of 1964.

I signed up for first year Chemistry at the University of Massachusetts, for some reason believing that my difficulty with high school Chemistry would no longer apply at the college level. One of the few tasks I performed correctly was purchasing a required kit of instruments, which included the aforementioned scissors, to use for the class.

Within a week or so, I cut my hand on a flask that I broke. I quickly dropped the course, but kept the scissors. At the time, I didn't realize the significance. Isn't that the way with many of life's events that seem meaningless at the time, but wind up affecting us for the rest of our lives.

These scissors weren't particularly useful, unless perhaps in the Chemistry class. The blades were small, about an inch, so they weren't good for cutting paper or anything of substance since they also weren't very strong.

But somehow they stayed with me through college, law school, one marriage, two children and about 10 moves. This fall we celebrated our 48th anniversary together.

I don't know when I first realized they were special, maybe 20 years ago, maybe 30. But at some point, decades ago, I looked at them and thought, I can't believe I still have these scissors.

I still wear the watch my uncle gave me for my high school graduation, which predated the scissors by only a few months. Although I take pride in wearing the same watch for 48 years, my still having that watch makes some sense. But outside of the watch, these scissors have been with me longer than any other possession. What are the odds?

I don't still have my baseball cards. And there are all kinds of other things from childhood and high school I wish I'd saved, but didn't have the foresight to do so. Television sets, cars, Beatles recordings in many formats have come and gone. During this time, who knows how many times my skin cells have completely regenerated. But these scissors remain, year after year.

I'm not sure what, if anything I used them for during their early years, but now they have a specific purpose. I use them to cut off the price tags on clothes. I suppose normal scissors would do that, but the small blades are ideal for the task.

Like most of us from 1964, the scissors are a little rusty, and they're not as sharp as they used to be, but if they ever break, it'll be a sad day. I imagine I'd try to get them repaired and if I couldn't, I'd be reluctant to just throw them away. In today's disposable society, I think it's important to be loyal to those who have been loyal to you.

I was only there briefly and I remember nothing from my college chemistry class. But I wonder how many of my classmates could honestly say they got as much out of the class as I did.

Faces fade to youth at reunion

I attended my 25th-year high school reunion last week in Brookline, Mass.

Over 500 were in my graduating class, and to give you an idea of my impact on the class of '64, my name appeared in the reunion booklet under the S's: Lexco, Stanley.

When I arrived I was struck by how old everyone looked, but as the evening wore on, the faces began to look more and more like they used to. It was as if some fairy godmother had allowed us to spend a few hours being 17 again.

I told Roy Swartz, who had no idea who I was, that I always think of him when I hear "All My Lovin'" by the Beatles, because I still have a clear memory of Roy raving about that song the day after the Fab Four appeared on TV.

Russell Franklin showed me the Class Will, which listed me as hoping to be the first lawyer to successfully defend Jack Ruby. Today, I attribute that ambition not so much as a desire to be a defense attorney but to demonstrate my affection for President Kennedy, a former Brookline resident who'd been slain a few months earlier.

When I encountered Peter Werwath, my first Brookline High friend, the first thing he said was, "Remember the time you gave me 8-1 on Clay vs. Liston and I collected 16 bucks?"

I suppose I would have preferred to be remembered for something more meaningful, but I'll concede it would be hard to find one incident that was more representative of me and 1964.

Our senior year, Louis Goverman, the incumbent class president, faced a challenge from Ron "Pimo" Pimental. Louie was upper-class, good-looking, college-bound. Pimo was none of the above.

Pimo lost in a close race, but almost all who voted for him did so as a goof that allowed us to show our evil side without risk.

A funny thing happened at the reunion. Louie's string of never attending a reunion remained intact, but Pimo was there. When Mike Stacy, the master of ceremonies, moved that we rectify our mistake from 25 years ago and elect Pimo president, the vote was unanimous.

And while the vote in '89 still had elements of a goof, I realized that we really did make a mistake in '64. The fact that Pimo cared enough to show up and Louie didn't, said it all.

It was nearing midnight and it was 1989 again. Stacy asked if we wanted to plan for our 50th in 2014. There was no response.

We knew how quickly the past 25 years had gone and we knew the next 25 would go even quicker. And maybe if we didn't plan for the next reunion, we could postpone facing the reality of how quickly it's all passing by.

When you're eating out these days, it's like a new world order

I don't know when it happened, but going out to eat these days is different from how it used to be.

A few years ago, it seemed like almost every server would physically lower themselves to take my order, as if getting down to my eye level would demonstrate some sort of familiarity or humility that would help me identify with them. That practice seems to have gone by the wayside and replaced by a new greeting.

"Hi. I'm Aaron. I'll be taking care of you tonight."

Really? You'll be taking care of me? I'm sorry. I must be in the wrong place. I thought I was going out to eat, but must have inadvertently made a wrong turn and wound up at a doctor's office, which has apparently installed a salad bar.

When my meal is finally nearing an end, I'm certain to be asked a question about dessert that they never used to ask. It seems to me there are a host of ways to accurately determine if a diner wants the meal to continue past the main course.

"Will that be all?", "Can I bring you anything else?", or maybe even something as simple as, "Would you like dessert?"

But no!

Invariably, it's, "Have you saved room for dessert?"

Is the answer to that question really going to be determinative? There are just so many variables. What if I didn't intentionally save room for dessert but, I'm still hungry, but I just don't want dessert. Is the answer to the question "yes" or "no"? There certainly have been times when I had plenty of room, but no desire. And sometimes even if I felt there was no vacancy, I stuffed it in anyway.

But the dessert question doesn't bother me nearly as much as the fact that waitresses (I know that's not a politically correct word) are starting to call me by what seems like inappropriately affectionate names, like 'hon', 'dear' and 'sweetie'. It may also be politically incorrect to say that I'm a little relieved that so far this has been confined to waitresses.

For a while, I couldn't figure out, why this sudden familiarity? They never used to call me those things. But it gradually dawned on me that I now appear so old or worse yet, am so old, that the waitresses know they have absolutely nothing to be concerned about. For them, they may as well be talking to a toddler.

How humiliating is that?

Obesity: Where does a 7,200-pound elephant sleep?

Every once in a while, a news story jolts me into thinking about things I never thought about before. I read just such a story last week.

Bunny, the only elephant at Mesker Zoo, has been put on a diet these past five years. She's slimmed down from an elephantine 7,840 pounds to a reasonably svelte 7,200.

In all my years on this planet, I had never once given a second thought to elephant obesity. But reading that article got me to thinking.

How do you tell if an elephant needs to lose weight? Do elephants have a recommended weight for a certain height? And if they do put on a few hundred extra pounds, does it all go to their hips?

Are some elephants blessed with a high metabolism rate so they can eat anything they want without putting on weight? And are those elephants the envy of the elephant world?

Are fat elephants sensitive about their weight? If so, why does it seem they never do anything about it?

Assuming Bunny even knows what she looks like, how could she know she's fat with no other thin elephant to compare with?

These questions bothered me, so I decided to call the zoo to get some answers, but after I received the information, all that happened was I thought of more questions.

I found out every few years the state police weigh her on the scales they use for weighing overweight trucks. I learned that Bunny was brought to Evansville from the wild when she was 2, about 33 years ago.

They're still feeding Bunny a lower grade of hay; which has fewer calories than the high-grade, because they want her to lose another 200 pounds. Then they may artificially inseminate her.

I wonder, for an elephant on a diet, are the last 200 pounds the hardest?

Does the local hay taste as good as the high-grade stuff?

If Bunny has a history of obesity, is her offspring more likely than the average elephant to suffer from the same problems.

If they've gone through all the trouble of slimming her down, presumably she's more attractive to a fellow elephant. If that's true, why use artificial insemination? Why not bring in the real thing? Could it be that after shedding nearly half a ton, bunny still wouldn't have any sex appeal?

I don't know the answers to any of these questions, but I do know that the next time I see an elephant, I'll be a lot more sensitive.

Marines at embassy
forgot their motto

In the wake of the marines sex-spy scandal, the Reagan administration is considering leveling our embassy and erecting a bug-free building. That still won't solve the problem.

Once the embassy is built, how are we going to prevent unpatriotic Marines from succumbing to the wiles of attractive Soviet women? Not long ago the phrases "unpatriotic Marines" and "attractive Soviet women" were oxymorons.

Arthur A. Hartman, a former ambassador to the Soviet Union, has a simple solution – replace the young, single Marines with "older, married" guards.

This may not be as easy as it sounds. Although it's common knowledge that older, married men are not interested in sex, it may depend on how much older and married are the Marines that Hartman is talking about.

Older, as I have learned the hard way, is a relative term. The misguided Marines in this case were in their 20s. I wonder if I would sleep more soundly knowing a 30-year-old Marine was standing guard and some sultry Soviet siren started caressing his cheek with her babushka – even if he was married.

Which brings me to my next point. Is being married really going to prevent a dalliance by a Marine? I used to think being an older, married evangelical minister was a guarantee of purity, but if they're susceptible, then no group, even the Marine Corps, is immune.

I know the Marines' motto is semper fidelis, but "always faithful" may be of little use if someone name Violetta starts whispering sweet propaganda in your ear.

And even if you can find marines old enough and married enough to resist temptation, I'd question whether those guys would be sufficiently alert to stop a Soviet spy from sneaking past them. Besides that, older, married men bring additional problems the younger, single ones don't have.

In the time it takes an older married man to take out the garbage, pick up his socks, clean out the garage or stop by the PX to get some bread and milk, the place would be crawling with bug planters. Because single men don't waste their time doing any of these tasks, they would not leave their post as often, limiting the opportunity for infiltration.

Guarding a new embassy with older, married men is definitely not the answer. What we ought to do is send the young, single guys back to basic training and teach them how to just say "nyet."

Arnold to Maria: 'It's not a rumor'

Arnold Schwarzenegger has written an autobiography, "My Unbelievably True Life Story." In the book and in an interview with "60 Minutes" on Sept. 30, Arnold tells the story of his unbelievable life, including details of what everyone wants to know about: his fathering of a child with his maid, Mildred, about the same time as he fathered a child with his wife, Maria. Not surprisingly, this ultimately led to the end of his 25-year marriage.

For more than seven years, Arnold managed to hide the fact from Maria that this child, who was living in his house with the maid, was his son. He only revealed it after Maria voiced her suspicions during a marriage counseling session.

When asked on "60 Minutes" why he didn't tell her sooner, Arnold explained, "I didn't know how to tell her."

I imagine most people watching that program were not satisfied with that answer. And while I am not defending Arnold's actions, I'd guess that if you've gotten yourself in that kind of predicament, figuring out how to tell your wife about it is a problem not easily solved.

I don't think offering flowers or candy beforehand would make the explanation more palatable, unless your wife really likes flowers or candy.

It's not just the content of the explanation you'd need to worry about. Timing could be key. Do you confess immediately, wait to see if the maid gets pregnant or, like Arnold did, wait until he's in school?

Sometimes the best defense is a good offense, but in this case, trying to shift the blame would not be a good idea. Even though you might conceivably get credit for confessing immediately, I doubt that beginning with, "Honey, you know how you're always pointing out how hard Mildred works and that we ought to do something special for her? Well, I realize this might not be what you had in mind, but yesterday…," is unlikely to go over well.

Similarly, if you waited until the child was born and said, "Maria, you know how sometimes you do something and as soon as you do it, you know it was a mistake? Well, nine months ago, I…" probably isn't going to be successful either.

Waiting for years isn't going to help much. Even if Maria commented on what a cute child he was, I don't think it would have gone smoothly if Arnold immediately replied, "I'm glad to hear you say that, Maria. I've had something I've been meaning to tell you for over seven years, but I've been waiting for the right moment and now seems to be the right time. I know you're going to find this incredible, but hear me out…"

These days when bookshelves are filled with "How To" books on just about everything imaginable, I'd venture to guess there isn't a single book or article that offers a good explanation of how to tell your wife you got the maid pregnant.

Maybe, it's because there isn't one.

When it rains, it pours comments on rubbers

"Nice rubbers, Stan."

"Does your mother make you wear those?"

"I just want to know one thing. Are you taking your rubbers to Indianapolis with you?"

These are just a few of the comments I've had to put up with this week simply because it rained and simply because I have the good sense to keep my feet dry by putting rubbers over my shoes.

Let's get the obvious snickering out of the way. It's impossible to say the word "rubbers" these days without thinking of those little things that used to be put in a wallet.

I thought by the time I hit 40-something, my contemporaries could talk about rubbers without winking, blushing or trying to make some pre-pubescent wisecrack. But I was wrong.

There's something about just hearing the word "rubbers" that propels otherwise dignified adults back to their teen-age years in the back seat of a Chevy.

Now that I hopefully have the snickering out of the way, permit me to return to the topic at hand: What's wrong with a guy wearing his rubbers when it's raining?

Rubbers have gotten a bad rap. I have the feeling that others think I'm not acting like a real man when I wear them.

Before George Bush changed his image, he would have been the kind of guy you'd expect to wear rubbers, but there's no way Ronald Reagan would try on a pair.

Alan Alda and Phil Donahue might wear them, but I'd be real surprised if Burt Reynolds or Bruce Willis did.

I'm not sure about Dustin Hoffman, but in know Robert De Niro wouldn't.

When I was younger, my mother did make me wear rubbers, but when I moved away from home I cast them aside. But then I noticed something.

When it rained, my shoes got wet. Sometimes when it rained real hard, the water soaked through my shoes into my socks and made my feet wet. I didn't like that, so I returned to my rubbers. Ever since my feet have been dry.

Most of my contemporaries are living more prudently these days. They exercise more. They've cut down on cholesterol. They don't drink and drive and they've undertaken a host of other practices that would make their mothers proud.

But they won't wear their rubbers, even though good hygiene and common sense says otherwise.

I'm tired of carrying on this crusade alone.

Maybe if they had athletes endorse rubbers it would help. Look what Michael Jordan has done for sneakers. Imagine what he could do for rubbers. Maybe Congress could pass a resolution recognizing a "Rubber Awareness Day."

Whatever plan is implemented, something needs to be done to encourage adult males to get their rubbers out of the closet and back on their feet where they belong.

It's an idea whose time has come.

Teaching the truth about justice

I am teaching Trial Advocacy at the Indiana Maurer School of Law and, although I've taught on various legal topics for more than a quarter century, this time it's different.

In the past, I've always focused on how to be an effective prosecutor. But now it's more universal.

Yes, I'm using my vast knowledge of trial tactics to give advice to not only prosecutor wannabes but to potential defense attorneys who may one day use something I said to thwart the noble plans of some fine upstanding God-fearing law-abiding society-protecting advocate for the people.

I realized that after decades of tailoring my advice to the prosecution, attempting to be neutral might pose a challenge. So for my first class, I asked a fellow instructor, whose day job is judge, to monitor my class to make sure I played it straight down the middle.

I divided the class in half, one half prosecuting a mythical case, the other acting as defense. We role-played various stages of the trial, with my giving helpful hints along the way, carefully measured in equal proportion to both sides. The hour flew by and when it was over I was confident I had managed to keep whatever bias I might have had in check.

"That wasn't so bad, was it?" more like stating than asking Judge Mary Ellen.

"No, it wasn't so bad," she replied, emphasizing the word "so" before continuing, "but there are a few things you might want to consider."

"Like what?" "Well, for starters, I think by dividing the class into 'good' and 'evil,' you send the wrong message."

"How so?"

"It kind of implies that it's a foregone conclusion the defendant is guilty. Perhaps you should have just said, 'prosecution' and 'defense.'"

"Point taken. Anything else?"

"When you were talking to the evil side, you said, your primary job is to get the best deal you can for your client."

"What's wrong with that?"

"Nothing, as far as it goes. But how about exploring the possibility that the client might not be guilty? Perhaps someone else committed the crime."

"I don't get it. What do you mean he 'might be not guilty'? Are we talking theoretical or real world here?"

"Both. And even if he committed the crime, the proof may be lacking. The defense should always be looking to raise a reasonable doubt."

"I guess you're right. Anything else?"

"Now that you mention it, when you were coaching the prosecutors, you told them to devise a coherent strategy and theme to prove their case, but when it came time for the defense, you asked them the best way to confuse the jury and wondered if they could think of any good tricks."

"Your point?"

"Well, until the trial's over, the defendant is presumed innocent. The jury has to assume he didn't do it, so until there's a verdict, both sides' strategy is equally legitimate. That's how the presumption of innocence works."

"I've always wondered why the judges keep harping on that instruction."

"And while I'm on the subject, you shouldn't have kept referring to the alibi as 'phony alibi' as if it were one word, phonyalibi. Every time you referred to the alibi, you prefaced it with 'phony'"

"What should I have said?"

"Simply say, 'alibi,' until the trial's over."

"Let me guess. The presumption of innocence thing, again?"

"Right. For all we know, his alibi might be true."

"Are you kidding? In all my years…"

"And another thing. Your word choice. When you said, that was a good argument—for a defense attorney, it left me with a bad taste."

"Did I do anything right?"

"Let me think a minute."

"C'mon. I must have done something right."

"Ok. I really liked the way you learned all your students' names so quickly"

"Is that it?"

"That and you started and ended on time."

"That's not much consolation. This is terrible. If the dean finds out, I'll be fired."

"Not to worry. My lips are sealed. They'll never be able to prove any of this. And the way I see it, you're…" She paused dramatically and motioned with her hands as if to drag the words out of me.

"Innocent until proven guilty," I sighed.

Death has a way of taking edge off feeling great about 40

Janis and Jimi died of drug overdoses, Thurman died in a plane crash, Natalie drowned and John was murdered.

But there's something about the death of "Pistol Pete" that is more frightening to us 40-ish males than the prospect of a call from Glenn Close inviting us to join her for a friendly drink after work.

Here's a guy just turned 40, in the prime of his life (which I used to think was 30), drug-, alcohol- and stress-free, playing a friendly pickup game of basketball, says he feels great and then keels over and dies.

It's like he died of old age.

I ran into my friend Hank the other night at Eastland Mall. Hank bid farewell to 40 a couple of years ago, yet you'd never know it by his activities – basketball, skiing and running in the winter, basketball and triathlons in the summer.

When I noticed him he was leaning against a wall with his right hand holding his left wrist.

"Hey, Henry. Long time, no see. What're you doing?"

"Checking my pulse."

"Why are you doing that?"

"Pistol Pete, man. It could happen to us."

"It's not gonna happen to you. You're in great shape. Are you feeling bad?"

"I feel great."

"Well, then, you've got nothing to worry about."

"That's why I am so worried. 'I feel great' is exactly what Pistol Pete said before he went plop."

"It's a fluke, Henry. People our age aren't really dying of natural causes."

"That's what you think. Try reading the obituaries like I started doing. Every day, someone in his 30s or 40s buys the farm. It's frightening."

"You're exaggerating. We've got plenty of good years left."

"Oh yeah? Have you noticed how old your high school classmates look lately?"

"Sure. But that's them, not us."

"Don't kid yourself, Stanley. One of these days, you'll be shoveling snow or mowing the lawn or just dribbling a basketball and the next day you're pushing up daisies."

"Don't be so morbid. You still play basketball and you're over 40."

"Played. I gave it up last week."

"How about triathlons this summer?"

"The only triathlon I'll be entering is the get-out-of-bed, take-a-shower, and put-on-your-clothes sweepstakes."

"Hey, I've heard enough of this. I've got to get going. I'll see you around."

"I'll be keeping my fingers crossed."

Dr. Brown's diet soda isn't place for warning

So there I was, in Shapiro's cafeteria in Indianapolis. I had taken my first bite of perhaps the best corned-beef sandwich in the state of Indiana and was raising my can of Dr. Brown's diet black cherry to my lips when what did I see on the label of the can?

"Use of this product may be hazardous to your health. This product contains saccharin which has been determined to cause cancer in laboratory animals."

It was not the sort of message I needed to read at that moment. I'd been looking forward to the sandwich all morning.

What was I supposed to do? I knew I couldn't properly enjoy the sandwich without a drink, but I also knew that getting up to buy another would send me crashing from corned-beef heaven.

I really needed more information before making my decision.

If the label had said, "Your chances of getting cancer are roughly equivalent to getting a congratulatory telegram from Ed McMahon," I would have had no problem.

On the other hand, if it had said, "Four-out-of-10 diet black cherry drinkers should have drawn out their IRA before they turned 50," I would have considered my options.

I also would have liked to have known what kind of laboratory animals they were talking about. I would have been a lot more uneasy if I had thought monkeys and gorillas were dropping like flies than if I had known rats and snakes were meeting their untimely demise.

I was thinking that they wouldn't have allowed it to be sold if it were really lethal – would they?

If they are really serious about giving a warning, they ought to do it before you buy the can. Once you've flipped the top and raised the can and discovered the message, it's too late.

Maybe they ought to divide the drinks into different sections before they're sold.

For example, they could put the ones that make you fat and prone to heart attacks in one section, the ones that cause cancer in another section and the ones that don't create problems but taste lousy in another section. At least you'd have fair warning.

If I wanted to scare someone to death, I'd be a little more graphic. Perhaps a cartoon of the deceased laboratory animal lying on its back in front of a gravestone labeled "R.I.P." with an empty can at his side would do the trick. Or maybe just a skull and crossbones would suffice.

But as I looked at this written warning, and considered my options, I decided they were bluffing.

Some people race hydroplanes. Others climb mountains. This week I drank a Dr. Brown diet black-cherry soda.

This odoriferous issue
might help clear the air

A headline on the front page of Wednesday's Courier grabbed my attention: "Couple, kicked off flight for BO, demand apology."

I don't think I've heard the term "BO" since I was in junior high school. Throughout my wonder years, accusing someone or being accused of having BO was an everyday kind of occurrence. But sometime in the '60s, terms like BO and halitosis vanished.

It wasn't that people stopped smelling bad; it's just that we started to refer to the problem indirectly, the way commercials did: "Aren't you glad you use Dial? Don't you wish everybody did?" as opposed to, "Since you began using Dial, you don't smell nearly as bad as you used to, but a lot of people still do."

Apparently USAir wasn't very subtle in kicking the couple off its plane. They wouldn't let the husband on another flight until he had washed up.

But his wife says there never was a problem. She says that on the next flight, she asked the woman next to her if they smelled, and the woman said no. So now the wife wants the price of two tickets from Los Angeles to New York.

I suspect that this is a case that even Judge Wapner would have difficulty resolving.

Even if the alleged smellers demonstrate that the woman said they didn't smell, what does that prove? If you were on a plane and two odoriferous strangers asked you if they smelled, what would you say? I'd be afraid to say anything that might make them mad.

Yet, how is USAir going to prove they really did smell? Unless they agree not to bathe for the trial, you can't preserve the odor. You can't bottle it and you can't take a picture of it.

I'm afraid USAir would be stuck with a variation of Justice Potter Stewart's description of pornography: "We can't describe BO, but we know it when we smell it."

I applaud USAir's efforts to clear the air. First the airlines went after the smokers. Now they're going after the smellers.

How could the skies be any friendlier than that?

Keeping track of mileage is helpful

"Is it true that you keep a record of all the miles you've ever run?"

I was asked this question recently by someone I had just met. Of all the reputations to have precede me, keeping track of all my running miles would not have been near the top of my list, assuming I kept a list of questions I would expect to be asked by someone first meeting me.

Actually, it's not literally true. I've only kept a record of every mile I've run for about the past 40 years, a few years after I began running.

But I could tell my questioner thought there was something unusual about such a practice. It seems normal to me. It's not as if I'm like Howard Hughes, who didn't cut his fingernails for years.

There are a number of qualities that I believe most great runners share: Speed, endurance and keeping track of their mileage. For me, to paraphrase Meatloaf, one out of three ain't bad.

Every January I break out a legal pad and, across the top, I write the year and my mileage goal for the year. And on the ensuing 10 sheets or so, I dutifully record every mile to the tenth. I'll also write down the times of races I ran and occasionally the weather or topography, if it's extreme.

In a world filled with subjectivity and events spinning out of control, recording the numbers is a way to keep some sense of objectivity and familiarity in my life.

How are things going? Was it a good year? Did I do all I should have done? These questions and others like them are difficult to answer with precision, but when someone asks me how many miles I've run this month or this year, I have a ready answer.

Sometimes the truth contained on the page can be difficult to handle. There was a period of time, a number of years ago, when my times in races stayed pretty steady, year after year. I convinced myself that although I was aging chronologically, since my times weren't getting any slower, I was successfully battling the aging process.

But those steady times of previous years are a distant memory. For a number of years now, there's been a gradual, sometimes more than gradual, steady decline. I know it's to be expected, but it's still frustrating. On the other hand, maybe if I didn't keep track, I might think I'm falling apart faster than I actually am.

I've had some injuries, which I also record, so this has been a low mileage year for me, just more than 500. In a few days, I'll get out a new legal pad and start the process all over again.

Assuming good health, I should be able to shatter this year's total next year. But one thing's for sure. If at the end of 2014, someone asks me if I'm running as much as I used to, I won't have to guess, because I'll have it all written down, every mile.

You got a problem with that?

CHAPTER

3

Shoe in middle of road is a foot over my head

Shoe in middle of road is a foot over my head

There are some things I am destined not to understand. I could live to be 200 and never understand electricity. The workings of almost any machine are beyond my comprehension. And why the Red Sox can't win the seventh game of a World Series will undoubtedly baffle me to my grave.

But I have the feeling if I just tried harder I could solve the mystery of the single shoe in the middle of the road. Recently I was driving on U.S. 41 and saw a woman's white shoe on the median. A few days later, I saw a gray running shoe in the middle of Lincoln Avenue.

Where do these shoes come from? Why is there always only one?

If you see rubbish on the side of the road, you can guess that some slob was too lazy to dispose of it in the proper manner. Or if you see a dead animal in the road, you can assume a car hit it. But how single shoes wind up there is beyond my comprehension.

I generally spot these shoes in the morning, and I wonder if there are people running around after dark shedding half of their footwear as some sort of bizarre cult ritual. Perhaps there's a podiatric equivalent of Johnny Appleseed.

Maybe they're the result of some pedestrian getting so mad at a driver that he takes a shoe off and throws it at a car. Or maybe it's a driver throwing his shoe at a pedestrian.

What happens to these shoes after they've been in the road for a while? Is there a special squad of shoe collectors that picks them up and puts them all in one place? If so, do they ever get a match?

I wonder if the owner ever retrieves one of these.

"Honey, do you have any idea where I could find my right brown loafer?"

"I'm not sure. Why don't you try the hall closet or under the bed, or if it's not there, check the southbound lane of Green River Road near Washington."

I wonder if the shoes are distributed in some kind of elaborate giant connect-the-dots pattern and if I followed their trail, I'd wind up at a shoe mecca, like The Carnival.

Maybe dogs drag them out there. Perhaps motorcycle riders lose them when they're making a quick start. I suppose mischievous kids could throw them out while their parents aren't looking.

If so many people are losing one shoe, why don't we ever see people wearing one shoe?

I'll probably never find the answer to any of these questions, but to all those people who own shoes, I say, if the shoe fits, don't leave it in the middle of the street.

Ex-penny-picker-upper
finds no sense in it

I was walking down the street the other day and there in the middle of the sidewalk was a penny.

Most people would have either picked it up or continued to walk, but I just stood there, unable to decide what to do.

It wasn't always this way. There was time when I wouldn't hesitate to pick up a penny. But for the last few years I've struggled with the concept.

More and more lately I've found myself looking for an excuse to pass it by. I won't pick up that one because it's too wet, scratched or dirty, I would rationalize.

If I did bypass a penny for no good reason, I'd feel guilty. Have I gotten so high and mighty that I'm too good to stoop down and pick up a penny, I'd ask myself rhetorically.

My mother takes a great deal of pleasure in finding pennies. She thinks it's lucky.

My daughter squeals with delight every time she finds one. She thinks she's found a treasure.   I'm afraid once she learns their value – or lack of value – she'll react more like her father than her grandmother. I suppose that's part of my problem.

A penny just isn't worth anything anymore.

Penny candy costs at least a nickel. And at some convenience stores, pennies are given away to assist customers in making exact change.

There seems to be a lot more pennies on sidewalks these days.

I wonder if that's because more pennies are actually finding their way to sidewalks or are they remaining there longer because fewer people are picking them up?

I wonder how they actually get there. Are they dropping out of pockets or are people throwing them away because they don't want them?

Whatever the answer, it wouldn't solve my immediate problem – what to do with the penny on the sidewalk. I stared at it. It stared back – not scratched, not wet, not dirty. But I just didn't feel like bending down and picking it up.

I stood there and thought about it. Suppose somebody offered me a dollar to bend down 100 times and pick up a penny – would I take the deal? I didn't think so.

How about if I were offered $10 to perform the task 1,000 times? Probably not.

I had my answer. If it wasn't worth $100 for 10,000 times, then it couldn't be worth one cent for one time. So I walked by that penny and resolved a philosophical conflict that's been troubling me for years.

But in my heart, I know my mother would not be proud.

Treasuring the right to not vote early

Vote early and vote often.

I never thought I'd do either, but earlier this week I was guilty of the former. Voting early is hardly illegal. In fact, it's encouraged by many of the candidates, who apparently assume you'll be voting for them. Even though I did it, I didn't feel good about it.

I have a feeble excuse. I have a meeting scheduled for Tuesday morning in Indianapolis. I could have postponed the meeting or rushed back in time to vote, but I took the easy way out. And voted early.

It wasn't the same. I missed seeing all the signs at the precinct place and even all the people handing out literature that I rarely pay attention to.

But not having them there detracted from the experience.

The first Tuesday after the first Monday in November is Election Day. That's the day voters are supposed to cast their ballots, not some random weekday in the fall. There used to be something special about Election Day, when all good citizens exercised their sacred right to participate in their democracy. Now, instead of Election Day, it's election season or whatever.

I'm a traditional kind of guy. I like things in their proper places.

If they suddenly announced it was all right to eat turkey any time within 10 days of the fourth Thursday in November, I wouldn't like it, even if it was more convenient.

I know I'm on the wrong side of history on this. While all states don't allow early voting yet, it is heading there. Oregon even allows voting by mail.

What's next? Voting by iPhone? I wish I were joking.

Because of the devastation of Superstorm Sandy, pretty soon they'll be passing a natural disaster exception for Election Day, probably followed by an inclement weather exception.

As this trend continues, more people will take advantage of early voting. In Ohio, there already are poll results of people who have voted early.

We used to worry about TV news calling the winners before polls in California closed. Soon, they'll be declaring a winner before polls open on Election Day. And, eventually, we can call Election Day what it is fast becoming: Vote Counting Day.

As much as I don't like where this is headed, with advancing technology I can imagine one possible advantage of early voting that would make me a convert.

What if, similar to a "Do not call" list, they could program your TV not to air campaign commercials as soon as you voted.

If that happens, look for me happily standing in line to vote sometime in June.

Monkey mating game zoo's view of success

News item – Atlanta zoo officials are planning to mate Willie B., a 30-year-old male gorilla, now that tests have determined that Willie is fertile. Until now, Willie has not even seen a female gorilla, but if all goes as planned, introductions will be made within three months.

I suspect when Willie finds out what they're planning for him, he'll have a few anxious moments.

**

"Willie, we're going to fix you up with a female gorilla tomorrow."

"Fix me up? Hey, I don't need any blind dates."

"Willie, we've waited 30 years and you haven't done anything on your own, so we had to do something."

"What does she look like? I bet she's got a great personality, right?"

"Well, she's 6 feet 2 inches tall, weighs about 270 and has hair all over her face and body."

"You're kidding. She sounds too good to be true. What's wrong with her?"

"Nothing. She comes from a fine family of gorillas but she thinks it's time to settle down and raise a pack of gorillas."

"What did you tell her about me?"

"Just that you like to swing from trees and pound your chest a lot. She can't wait to meet you."

"I just hope she doesn't think I'm too primitive. I'm afraid I won't even know what to say."

"Just don't say anything cute like she's the gorilla of your dreams or you think you're going ape over her. I guarantee you, she's heard them all a hundred times."

"What should I say then?"

"Be yourself. Just act natural. You might want to break the ice with a gift of flowers and bananas. No gorilla can resist that."

"What should we do?"

"How about dinner? It's a good way to get to know someone."

"I'm afraid my table manners have gotten a little rusty, living alone all these years. I always make a lousy first impression."

"Don't worry. There are only a few basic rules to keep in mind. Don't chew with your mouth open. Try not to talk about yourself the whole time. And don't sit on your food."

"What should I say after dinner?"

"Tell her you love the way she smells, the way she combs the hair on her legs, the sexy way she walks close to the ground."

"What else?"

"Tell her she's like no other female you've ever met."

"I've never met another female."

"She doesn't have to know that."

"What if she doesn't like me?"

"No way. You've got a certain animal attraction that's bound to drive her wild."

'Stan Levco is 40 today!' How, where, is he handling it?

Lauderdale-by-the-Sea, Fla.–I'm writing this column in anticipation of Sunday, June 15, 1986, presumably the day you're reading it. That's the day I hit the big four-oh, enter my fifth decade, leave my 30s forever and celebrate my 40th birthday.

This column won't be particularly funny because there's nothing particularly funny about turning 40. But I wanted to publish something on the topic, because when you get to be my age, you start thinking about leaving something of yourself behind for future generations.

I don't know the right way to commemorate the occasion, although I have a pretty good idea what I'll do. I'm sure I know some of the wrong ways, which is one of the reasons I chose this week to vacation in Florida.

I definitely don't want to see a billboard proclaiming, "Stan Levco is 40 today!" or a cute little ad in the newspaper with one of my boyhood pictures, or take a chance on a surprise party if I stayed in town.

It seems to me that one shouldn't turn 40 with a bunch of people asking, "So, what's it like to be 40?" When I return I'll handle it, but I don't want to have to deal with it on the day itself.

I turned 30 about 10 years ago, and I did it very badly. Hopefully, I've learned from my mistakes. Susie was playing bridge and I couldn't convince any of my friends to celebrate with me, so I stayed home watching TV, and stuffing myself with potato chips and ice cream.

I think I'll spend my 40th playing tennis in the morning, at the racetrack in the afternoon and dining on two lobsters at night with Susie, who's promised not to play bridge, and our friends Gail and Harry, who abandoned Evansville for Florida last year.

Being around tennis courts, race horses, lobster, Susie and friends isn't the only reason I expect 40 to be a lot easier than 30.

The concept of 30 was very difficult for me to accept. I was afraid of leaving my youth behind and I struggled to prevent middle age. I ran marathons, listened to Michael Jackson and for years resisted opening an IRA.

But it didn't do any good. I kept getting older at what seems like a progressively faster rate.

At 40, I'm not longer struggling against middle-age. I'm there.

A Yale University professor recently concluded that although the average American life expectancy has increased by about three years during the past two decades, it still is only about 70 for an American male. At 30, I could reasonably expect to have most of my life ahead of me. Now I know I'm probably closer to the end than the beginning.

I still have some resistance left. I take a certain amount of vicarious pleasure in the accomplishments of Rose, Abdul-Jabbar, Nicklaus and Shoemaker. And when I meet someone born around 1946, I don't care which one of us makes more money, but I am happy if I think I look younger.

But for the most part, I'm coming to terms with being 40, I take some comfort in the fact that as a Baby Boomer, there are so many others my age that I don't have to do this alone and I don't have to worry that my generation will ever be forgotten by advertisers or politicians.

And while I'm not happy about how quickly it's all passing by, on Sunday night – tonight – I'll gladly drink a toast to the fact that I'm still around to watch it.

Let Stan be Stan and not Bob – and vice versa

About thirty years ago, I wrote a column about being mistaken for Bob Pigman, hoping that writing about it would somehow help end the confusion. Little did I know, it was just the beginning.

At the time, we were both prosecutors. He was the elected prosecutor. I was a deputy. My complaint then was, I was always being mistaken for him, but never the other way around. While I didn't like it, given that he was a public official and clearly better known, it made sense that more people would mistake me for him than vice versa.

That was 30 years ago, and despite my getting elected to public office, appearing on TV periodically and writing this column, the disparity has not improved. If anything, it's become worse.

Last week, at Judge Shively's swearing-in, I was greeted by a photographer.

"Hi, Bob."

"I'm not Bob."

"Robert, then."

In what has become a mantra of sorts for me, I replied, "I am not Bob Pigman."

Need I say, I know this photographer. He knows me. I've hired him on numerous occasions. And he does not know Bob.

I sat down next to a guy who looked familiar. He introduced himself and explained how he knew me. "We used to run in races together," he explained.

When the ceremony was over, he said, "It was good to see you, Bob."
"I am not Bob Pigman."

Is it necessary to add that Bob did not run in any races with him and that during the ceremony the real Bob Pigman was introduced to the audience as an attending judge?

I wish I could say it surprised me. Two separate times, Bob and I have been eating lunch together and I was approached by a stranger calling me "Bob." I had to point out that the real article was sitting at the table next to me. Recently, when we were at lunch, a waitress mistakenly referred to me as "Judge." I asked if she thought we looked alike. She replied that she thought we were twins.

I've had relatives of his mistake me for him, and on more than one occasion I've had strangers interrogate my children, trying to force them to confess I was really Bob. One time, my denial prompted this irritated response: "Well, you used to be when you were in high school."

Although neither of us thinks we look alike, there are some unusual, nonphysical similarities. My career path — civil attorney, chief deputy prosecutor, judge, deputy prosecutor and elected prosecutor — is not a whole lot different from his: chief deputy prosecutor, elected prosecutor, civil attorney, deputy prosecutor and judge. We each have an eldest daughter named Jessica, and perhaps more significantly, both of us are certain that Lee Harvey Oswald acted alone.

The visual confusion isn't the only thing. We've each been mistaken for the other over the phone by our secretaries, which makes even less sense, given that Bob is a native Hoosier and I grew up working on a New England accent my first two decades.

I suppose it could be worse. It's not as if I'm being mistaken for Charles Manson. But I find it irritating that it happens so frequently, as if somehow I'm not a legitimate me. And even worse, it happens so much more to me than him. It happens to me at least once a month. He says it's only happened to him a handful of times.

How can this be? Do I look like him, but he doesn't look like me? The fact that it rarely happens to him makes it doubly frustrating. After three decades, I've learned to accept it, but that doesn't mean I have to like it.

If you see Bob in the next few days, tell him he looks like me. After I've lived with this for so long, that would seem like a small price for him to pay.

**Levco on left, Pigman on right, Evansville Mayor
Lloyd Winnecke in background**

Is father's attitude about care healthy?

Editor's note: *Jessica Levco is filling in for her father this week. She originally wrote this column for Ragan.com.*

My dad has diverticulitis.

I don't know anybody else who has this, but he says when I get to be his age, all my friends will have it.

Basically, his stomach hurts. And lately, it has been hurting him – a lot. A week and a half ago at 3:30 a.m., he was in so much pain, he drove himself to the ER. He didn't want to wake up my mom because she was sleeping.

When the results from his scans came back, his doctor called him in for an appointment. His doctor said he needed to have surgery immediately. My dad said, "OK." He met his surgeon, who seemed "nice."

When Dad was telling me about this, I couldn't help but interrupt him. I think our conversation highlights the differences between millennial and boomer health care consumers. The millennial wants to know and ask everything – the boomer will do as the doctor says and isn't too concerned about looking online for more information.

Here are a few conversation highlights:

"What are they going to do to you?"

"I don't really know," he said. "The surgeon used some fancy word, but I think he just meant they were going to cut out a piece of my colon."

"Is it cancer?"

"I can't remember anything they said, but I don't think so," he said. "I think if they would've said cancer, I might've remembered that."

"Are you going to die?"

"Oh, probably not," he said, with a melodramatic sigh. "But who knows? Que sera sera."

Que sera sera.

My dad is probably a lot like other boomers who are facing a major medical issue. He's not asking for a second opinion. He's not on Yelp or HealthGrades, researching hospitals or doctors. He has only told a handful of friends – reluctantly – about this. His doctor told him he needed to have surgery, and that's what he's going to do. No questions asked (literally, I don't think he asked any questions).

Here's the part in the story where I should give helpful tips to those marketing a hospital to this kind of audience, but really, I don't know how any of marketing efforts can reach someone like my dad.

A millennial, on the other hand, would handle my dad's situation completely differently. Right after seeing the doctor, we'd be Googling every term the doctor just said, taking meditation classes to prepare for surgery and reading reviews about our chosen hospital on Yelp, wondering if we're making the right decision.

And another major difference: If anybody my age was having surgery, they'd tell everyone through a text, blog, tweet or Facebook post. Case in point: I'm telling everyone about my dad's surgery.

My dad doesn't know what kind of surgery he's getting; he has a vague idea of what's being removed, but his main concern is if his doctors will let him drink milkshakes after it's over.

But the more I think about it, maybe the fact that he's not researching and not knowing what he's getting himself into is OK. He seems to be in good spirits and not panicked. He's just doing what he's told to do by a medical professional and hoping for the best. This is a foreign concept to my generation, but maybe it's just an easier way to live life.

However, my younger sister called me last night, upset and concerned about the surgery. She is expecting the worst. Here's her hypothetical scenario:

"If Dad dies, I don't think Mom will be able to go on without him," she says. "Mom will probably kill herself. If she kills herself, I'll kill myself, too. Then, you can write a book about it."

I told this to my mom.

She laughed and said, "I think your sister needs to be on medication."

Final post-surgery note from Stan Levco:

I'm writing this note five days after the operation. Those of you who read my column two weeks ago (about how I am often mistaken for Bob Pigman) may find it of interest that as I was about to be wheeled into the surgery, my respiratory therapist mistook me for Bob Pigman.

I am happy to report the operation was apparently a complete success. I will no longer suffer from diverticulitis. Not so with being mistaken for Bob Pigman. I'll have that condition for the rest of my life.

All things considered, not a bad trade.

Not ready for prime time

I've always wondered what it would be like to be a Talking Head, not the David Byrne type, the kind of guy that Piers or Matt or Katie would turn to when they want the inside scoop of what's going on in that trial.

I've waited long enough to be recruited and the call has never come, so I decided to nudge the process a little. Unbelievably, Talking Heads was listed in the Yellow Pages right between Talking Dogs and Talking Pictures, so I called the number and soon found myself talking to the head of Talking Heads.

"Hello, my name's Stan Levco and I'd like to apply to be a Talking Head on criminal law. I've watched all your people talking about what charges should be filed, whether there will be a plea, the trial strategy and the meaning of the verdict and I think I could do just as well or better," I said.

"Hold on, sir. It's not as easy as it looks. Our people are trained professionals. What makes you think you can do this?" replied the head Talking Head.

"I'm a fast learner and I'll give it 100%."

"Right off the bat, we've got a problem. Most of our people give it 110%, sometimes even more, but I suppose if you're what we're looking for we can waive the minimum percentage standard. What kind of experience do you have?"

"I've got a lot of courtroom experience. I've been trying cases for about 40 years and I've tried about 200 jury trials and I've had my share of favorable results," I said, straining to sound modest, while conveying the appropriate measure of success.

"Whoa. Jury trials? We're not looking for commentators with actual jury trial experience."

"You're not?"

"No. We prefer our people have little or no courtroom experience. That way, their personal experience doesn't get in the way of offering interesting observations about what happened in someone else's case."

"I can see that. But I'd be willing to do my best to not let my experience color my observations. Can't you at least give me a chance?"

"I suppose. Let me try a hypothetical situation on you and see how you react."

"Ask me anything."

"All right. Now we go to Stan Levco, who's on location outside the courthouse. Stan, the jury's been out for two days now. Does this favor the prosecution or defense?"

"How the... should I know?"

"Oh no, Stan. You can't say that on TV."

"I'm sorry, but can't you just bleep it out?"

"It's not the word, it's the thought. You said you didn't know. We're not going to be paying you to give mushy answers. You've got to say it's either good for the prosecution or the defense. Pick one. We don't care. Just as long as you take a position. And you can feel free to change it in mid-sentence. That's the beauty of being an expert on TV."

"What if the situation is such that there's no way of giving an informed opinion?"

"Are you kidding me? Don't you get it? We don't care if it's an informed opinion just as long as it's an opinion. The more extreme, the better. Face it. You're just not cut out for this line of work. Only a select few have what it takes," he said, letting me know the interview was over.

"I guess you're right," I concluded, reluctantly accepting the fact that I'm simply not ready for prime time.

If Gator's my co-pilot, just don't tell me

Consumer complaints about the airline industry are skyrocketing. Elizabeth Dole, secretary of transportation, warned that unless the airline industry begins to straighten up and fly right, the federal government might jump on board and impose new restrictions on airlines.

I have a few suggestions for the airlines that might help them avoid future complaints.

The pilots should avoid sounding too chummy. This week I took a flight where the pilot announced his name was Bubba and his co-pilot was Gator.

Bubba and Gator sound like a couple of guys I would have liked to drink with in college, but I'm not sure I trust them in the cockpit. I'd prefer my pilots were Harold and Edward. If it's Bubba and Gator, I'd rather not know.

Don't force the flight attendants to point to the exits or demonstrate how to breathe in the event an oxygen mask is needed. I feel sorry for them, when they're pointing, because no one ever pays attention. Why not have a show of hands to see if anyone wants instructions on the exits or the oxygen masks. If no one does, don't do it.

Don't tell passengers to "breathe normally" in the event oxygen is needed. Let's face it, if you need a mask, you'll be lucky to remember how to breathe at all, much less normally.

Eliminate the euphemisms for "crash." On the Bubba-Gator flight, the voice on the loudspeaker gave instructions in the event a landing on water was necessary.

Whom are they trying to kid? I know we're not going to make a fuel stop in the middle of the ocean and we're surely not going to drop off any passengers who need to make a connection on a cruise line.

The only way we're going to have a water landing is if we're plunging into the sea. And if we're crashing, I don't think familiarity with a flotation device will make much of a difference, anyway.

Identify the food that is served. Invariably my "snack" – they never have "meals" anymore – includes some strange foodstuff that I'm not familiar with. It would help if all food was labeled.

Tell us we're going to "experience a little turbulence" before the turbulence, not after. It seems they always wait until it's over before they tell you what happened. I'd like to be able to prepare myself.

Improve the exiting procedure. When we get on the plane, we board in single file. But when the plan stops, everyone jumps into the aisle and stands there for minutes until the passengers gradually exit. I'd prefer a procedure, like in weddings, where no one leaves until he's given permission by an usher.

Following the suggestions won't cure the airline industry overnight, but it could make the skies a lot friendlier.

Elephant, donkey, and now chicken?

Last week was a tough week for me and fast food.

What caused my difficulty was that Chick-fil-A President Dan Cathy issued a statement saying he was guilty as charged for backing the biblical definition of a family.

As you may imagine, this statement did not go over well in the gay community. As a result, mayors of New York, Boston, Chicago and San Francisco have removed the welcome mat for construction of Chick-fil-A restaurants in their cities. In response, Chick-fil-A supporters organized an Appreciation Day to counteract the bad publicity.

And here I am squarely in the middle. What's a gay-rights supporting Chick-fil-A aficionado supposed to do?

I eat a lot of fast food and I have my favorites. Chick-fil-A is at or near the top of my list. I love its sandwiches, nuggets, waffle fries and on occasion, its hand-spun milkshakes. (Before Chick-fil-A, I never even heard of a hand spun milkshake. And I'm still not sure exactly what it is, although it sounds impressive.)

I used to think being a supporter of gay rights and eating at Chick-fil-A was not mutually exclusive, but now I'm not so sure.

These days, when you're taking your life into your hands by going to a movie, there are fewer and fewer activities remaining where you can forget about the world's problems and just relax and enjoy things.

Until recently, I counted eating chicken nuggets as one of those carefree activities. It seems counterintuitive that eating or not eating chicken is now a political statement.

And yet, I know it's not so simple. If a restaurant had a picture of Adolf Hitler on the wall and its waitresses wore swastikas, I wouldn't think twice about taking my business elsewhere, no matter how good the food was. So I can't say the owners' philosophy has no bearing on my patronage. I guess it's a matter of degree.

In this case, all I know is this owner is against gay marriage and he had the bad business judgment to publicly state his beliefs. It would be different if he said he wouldn't hire gays or made potential customers sign a heterosexuality pledge.

Before I go into a Mexican restaurant, do I need to find out where the owner stands on immigration before I order a taco? Or the next time someone asks if I want fries with that, should my answer be, That depends on what your boss thinks about health care. If I withheld my business from every restaurant owner who disagrees with me on some issue, I would have to learn how to cook for myself and that would not be a good thing.

It's been a struggle, but I've decided, barring any new revelations that I can't rationalize, I will continue to enjoy my Chick-fil-A visits without guilt.

For me, it comes down to this: I believe in the separation of church and chicken.

Desire to finish school poses some questions

Princeton High School's student body may soon include Debra Murphree, the woman who led to the downfall of TV evangelist Jimmy Swaggart.

She currently is on a nationwide tour to promote her pictorial in this month's Penthouse magazine.

Ms. Murphree says she intends to return to her native Gibson County, re-enroll in high school and maybe become an interior designer.

I must confess that my first impression of her was not a positive one – and not simply because she was a prostitute. It was because she described her john, or in this case her jimmy, as "cheap and quick."

It seems unfair to describe a guy as cheap if he's paying what you're charging.

But what is worse is referring to him as quick. I can forgive her for trying to earn a living, and I certainly don't blame her for selling her story and posing for Penthouse, because of the money. But hadn't she done enough harm to Swaggart's reputation without telling the whole nation he was quick.

While I hope I'm never publicly accused of either, I think I'd rather be called a thief than be charged with being cheap and quick.

Reaction in the Princeton community to Ms. Murphree's return has been mixed.

When told that Ms. Murphree was planning to return to school, Principal Larry Ramsey said, "Oftentimes, when people say they're going to return to school, they mean they are going to get their GED."

Call me cynical, but I thought I detected a wisp of wishful thinking.

Let's assume it's not a GED she's interested in, but she intends to matriculate at Princeton High. Will she really fit in there?

What could possibly teach her that she doesn't already know? It seems to me in any economics, photography, biology or religion class, the student might be more knowledgeable than the teacher.

Somehow I just can't picture her as secretary of the Future Homemakers of America or sitting in detention because she was late for class. When I try to visualize her going door to door selling candy to raise money for a class project, something just doesn't seem right.

I wonder how a father would feel when his 16-year-old son comes home and says, "Hey, dad, can I borrow the car? I met this really neat girl named Debra. She's a little older than me, but I really like her."

I wonder if a mother would really feel comfortable sending her daughter to Ms. Murphree's house for an overnight slumber party.

Still, if she wants to continue her schooling, she ought to do it. I just think it's easier said than done.

HIGH SCHOOL

Getting nostalgic about misery

I got one of those good news/bad news diagnoses last week.

The good: Your recent surgery was successful. You won't need another colonoscopy for seven years and that will be your last one.

The bad: The reason that will be your last one is because after then, you'll be so old that if we found something wrong with you, you won't be worth operating on.

Those weren't my doctor's exact words, but pretty close.

Only having to contemplate one more colonoscopy should be cause for celebration. While I have no doubt the procedure is necessary and can prevent colon cancer, it is a wretched experience.

Virtually everyone who has undergone this procedure says the same thing: It's not the procedure, it's the preparation.

That's because you're under anesthetic during the procedure and other than feeling loopy, it doesn't hurt afterward. However, it's "before" that gets you.

You have to drink prodigious amounts of a liquid that you mix with something such as Gatorade to kill the taste, which isn't too bad at first but after the third or so glass, it's hard to get down. But that's not the worst part. Without going into too much detail, the results of this excessive drinking are many, many trips to the bathroom for many, many hours.

They can put a man on the moon. They can invent an iPhone and Kindle, but apparently no one can figure out how to mask the taste of this awful preparation or figure out a painless way to inspect your colon.

I've had about four of these preparations and colonoscopies over the years, the most recent being immediately preceding my surgery in March and each time I thought, "I dread having to go through this miserable experience again."

But a strange thing happened when I discovered the next one will be my last. Now that I'm going to be too old for a colonoscopy, my attitude toward the procedure is changing. I'm starting to feel downright nostalgic about the prospect. I know it's seven years away, but although that may be a long time in dog years, it's really not that far away.

There are too many significant things in life that we don't have the luxury of knowing when it's the last time – activities that we'll never do again, places we'll never visit again and people we'll never talk to again.

Not so for me and colonoscopies. Next time I drink that horrible liquid and next time I take repeated trips to the bathroom, I'll know it'll be my last.

I'm having serious mixed emotions about the prospect. When the time comes, will I be happy it's my last one so I won't have to suffer another one? Or will I be sad because I'm too old to suffer through another one?

Will I complain every few minutes because of how miserable I feel? Or will I savor and embrace every moment, happy that I'm still worthy of being put through the misery?

But I'm getting ahead of myself. Instead of wondering about how I'll deal with something in 2020, I just need to live in the moment and appreciate the next seven years, while I'm still arguably worth saving.

CHAPTER

4

Running for office from 20 points behind

Running for office from 20 points behind

I am running for my sixth term as prosecutor. You might assume that one who has been elected five previous times would enjoy the process or at the very minimum, be very good at it. If you did assume that, you would be wrong, that's for sure.

I view running for election about the same as I view the prospect of having a colonoscopy. It's something I have to do periodically. I worry about it, but I think it'll turn out ok, since it always has in the past. And it's always such a relief when it's over.

But with a colonoscopy, you can be unconscious for most of it. With a contested election, it's preferable to be awake and coherent, although being aware of what's going on can be very depressing.

Even though I've been doing this for a long time, I haven't acquired much political skill over the years, but I made a few observations that could be of assistance to those of you contemplating taking the plunge in electoral politics.

You get no credit for winning cases.

You only get blame for losing them. People expect prosecutors to win cases, so when they do, it's no big deal. You can try bragging about all the cases you've won—and I do whenever I can—but the public is far quicker to criticize a not guilty verdict than praise a conviction. Take the recent Rod Blagojevich trial—please. The prosecutor, Pat Fitzgerald was second-guessed in the media for his "unsuccessful" prosecution when all he did was convict a sitting governor of a felony while the jury hung 11-1 for conviction on the other charges. He was one juror away from a spectacular result, yet his tactics were criticized and his efforts were considered a failure. So when you hit the campaign trail, don't expect anyone beyond your immediate family to be impressed with your guilty verdicts.

No good deed goes unpunished.

I've stopped counting the times that I've bent over backwards for people for whom I've achieved great results, who supported my opponent because of some imagined slight or because of a result that may not have been 100% of what they wanted—which leads me to my next point.

Two out of three is bad. In his classic album, *Bat Out of Hell,* Meat Loaf sang, "Two out of three ain't bad." That's generally true in life, but not in prosecution. Who do you think people will vote for, if you've made two decisions that they're happy with and one decision that made them unhappy? Trust me. It ain't you.

Family members are something less than objective when evaluating how you should treat their relatives.

For some strange reason, most people's philosophy on criminal law has no relationship to their relations. The majority of hard liners just can't seem to understand why you don't think their son deserves a third chance at counseling.

Perhaps recognizing that people expect special treatment for their family doesn't qualify as a shocking revelation. But what continues to amaze me is how they rarely recognize the hypocrisy of asking for favorable treatment. And if you don't agree to give special consideration, you could end up paying the price at the ballot box.

If you thought you were finished with high school, think again.

You might think you are past the time when whether you've snubbed someone by not saying hello across a crowded room is a cause for concern or whether or not your handshake was firm enough or too firm or whether or not your opponent's yard sign is better than yours or whether you have enough Facebook friends or are tweeting enough. This may seem trivial, but a deficiency in one of these areas could have you starting a career in civil practice sooner than you intended.

There's no end to the advice you will get, much of which is incomprehensible and contradictory.

One of my favorite pieces of advice is, "Run like you're 20 points behind." What exactly does this mean? Is there a difference between running like you're 20 points behind or one point behind? And assuming you really thought you were 20 points behind, wouldn't you tend to get reckless and do extreme things that could cost you the election? If I'm Peyton Manning and I've got the ball on the 50-yard line with time running out and a lead, am I going to take a knee or make believe I'm behind and throw a Hail Mary?

If I really thought I was 20 points behind, I'd start planning for my next job instead of wasting my time on a futile campaign.

Don't predict the outcome of your race because people will disagree with you.

When asked what I thought would happen in the election, I used to reply, "I'm pretty confident of winning!" When I said that, people were offended and the inevitable reply would be, "You need to be worried. You can't take the race for granted. Anything can happen!" This would often be followed by the advice to "Run like you're 20 points behind."

So at some point I decided to change my answer to, "I'm worried. I'm not taking the race for granted. Anything can happen." When I said that, the response would generally be, "Are you kidding me? You're a shoo-in. There's no way you can lose. But you still need to run like you're 20 points behind."

So I learned that the best response to the question of "What do you think will happen?" is, "I don't know. All I know is I'm going to run like I'm 20 points behind."

A prosecuting attorney
is exactly who I am

For those of you who read my last column discussing the perils of running for election and are wondering how I did; I have two words which sum up the result: Tsunami and Democrat. (In the previous sentence, "and" does not count as a word.)

I should have seen it coming but I ignored the warning signs.

If I had listened more carefully to the responses, going door to door should have convinced me what was about to happen.

I am not a natural door-to-door kind of guy. I rarely began an outing thinking, "I can't wait to get out there, so I can disturb a bunch of strangers to tell them I'd appreciate their vote."

But once I started knocking it wasn't so bad, other than the fact the most common response I received was, "Sorry, I'm voting Republican." Someone without blinders on might have taken that as a hint that I was about to be buried in a Republican landslide. But I just blithely continued marveling at how amazing it was that the only people who opened the door just happened to be Republicans.

One of my most interesting encounters had nothing to do with my political affiliation. One time, a couple of barking dogs called my attention to a potential voter in a fenced yard across the street. I approached the woman, handed her a brochure from over the fence and said, "I'm Stan Levco. I'd appreciate your vote in November."

She stared coldly and said, "I know who you are," paused a moment and concluded, "I know exactly who you are."

In that millisecond, I understood the enormous difference between someone knowing who I was and someone knowing "exactly" who I was. I quickly made my way back across the street, but I could hear her say to her barking dogs, who also seemed to know exactly who I was, "You don't like Mr. Levco, do you?"

The blogs should have been another clue about what was to happen. I first became aware of blogs during the previous election when even a routine newspaper article about me would unleash a torrent of vicious criticism of me, both personal and professional. Some of it was even untrue.

So when it happened again this election, I didn't think it was cause for concern. My strategy for dealing with the blogs was to avoid reading them, but occasionally (Ok, most of the time), I couldn't resist.

I'll admit the ones I read this time seemed to be greater in volume and venom than before. There's one I can't seem to forget. "I waited on Levco many years ago and he was a lousy tipper."

C'mon! A lousy tipper? I can understand saying I prosecute innocent people, I don't prosecute guilty people or that I'm unethical. But how low do you have to be to anonymously accuse someone of being a bad tipper?

I always tip between 15 and 20 percent, even for bad service. My daughter once worked at a buffet, so I even routinely tip at buffets. I realize this doesn't make me eligible for the Tipper's Hall of Fame, but to be forever branded in the blogosphere as a cheapskate is not what I signed up for when I ran for public office.

So, what's next for me? And more importantly, will I continue to write this column?

I don't think I should, unless I'm still involved in prosecution. As of this writing, I haven't decided, but Indiana has a senior prosecutor statute that allows a former prosecutor to serve as a special prosecutor when the elected prosecutor has a conflict.

If I do continue to be a prosecutor, it'll be because it's who I am. In fact, it's exactly who I am.

Yesterday fills lonely heart of aging 'Sgt. Pepper'

This past week, the media has tried to tell us that "it was 20 years ago today" that the Beatles released "Sgt. Pepper's Lonely Hearts Club Band."

After a great deal of thinking about this, I can categorically state that it wasn't 20 years ago. Perhaps they made it up to get publicity for the new "Sgt. Pepper" compact disc. I don't know. But I do know it wasn't that long ago.

I was there. I remember it happening. I clearly remember going to the campus bookstore and buying it soon after it was released.

The night before the purchase, I shared a $25 first prize in my college dormitory talent contest for singing "Second Hand Rose" with two other friends who also spent more time memorizing lyrics than studying.

I'm not being overly modest when I say we weren't what you'd normally think of as a first-prize act. I suspect our winning was more attributable to our competition than our talent – only one other group entered and they were drunk.

It seemed appropriate that I spent my newly won $8.33 on the Beatles' new album. I'm sure it couldn't be 20 years since then.

I remember the shock of seeing the mustachioed quartet in shiny new band uniforms. I recall, on first hearing, how unusual the music was, but knowing that if that's where the Beatles were, that's where we were going. There's no way that all happened 20 years ago.

Since the album was released, we've had the Vietnam War, Watergate, the Iran hostages and now Ronald Reagan. I'm sure that's only been about 9 or 10 years, 12 tops.

If it really were two full decades ago, that would make me twice as old now as I was then. I don't feel twice as old. And I'm certainly not twice as wise.

The calendar has a very strange way of distorting the truth. It keeps claiming all these years have slipped by, when I know they haven't.

It certainly doesn't seem like 20 years ago that Sgt. Pepper was released. It seems like yesterday.

I don't believe in 20 years ago. I believe in yesterday.

Everybody looks good at 20th college reunion

Last weekend I went to my 20-year reunion at the University of Massachusetts. I also attended my 10-year reunion, but this one was different.

In 1978, we thought we could still pass for college students. We were just starting to settle into careers and we joked a lot about being middle-aged.

This time, some of us were parents of college students.

And middle age was no longer funny. It was reality.

This time, the class of '68 was much too sophisticated to be impressed with things like money or power. The only thing that mattered now was how young (or old) you looked.

I heard more people in one hour tell me I looked good than in the past 15 years in Indiana, which leads me to a number of possible conclusions:

Beauty being in the eye of the beholder, perhaps my looks are more appealing to Bay Staters than Hoosiers; maybe I get better looking the closer I get to the Atlantic; perhaps people in Indiana are just too reserved to tell me the truth; or maybe I don't really look that good, but the class of '68 has reached the age where saying "You look good" has about as much meaning as "Have a nice day."

To me the ultimate compliment was "Levco, you look exactly like you used to." It's strange I should have felt so flattered because I'm not being modest when I confess that 20 years ago no one ever accused me of being good-looking.

But realizing how much I enjoyed hearing it, I started saying it to others. To those who had aged badly, I'd say, "You're looking pretty good."

To those who looked their age, I'd say, "You look great."

And to those I recognized without a name tag, I'd say, "You really look great. I really mean that. Really."

It was more difficult for some than others. One guy approached me with an outstretched hand: "Hey, it's me, Charlie Hopkins. You haven't changed a bit, Stan."

"You're looking pretty good yourself, Charlie." (What happened to your hair?)

"Well, I've lost a lot of hair."

"Yeah, but it's hardly noticeable." (I suppose you could say you lost a lot of hair, but only if you consider 100 percent a lot.)

The highlight of the weekend was the dance. I spent more time than I care to admit choosing exactly the right clothes.

I arrived reasonably dressed and reasonably on time. The band played a lot of '60s music – stuff like "Louie, Louie," "Gimme Some Lovin'" and "Wooly Bully."

I didn't dance. I just stood and watched, and tried not to act conspicuous. Some things never change.

2004 Democratic Convention

Editor's note: Following are excerpts from columns written as a delegate to the 2004 Democratic Convention in Boston.

Monday–The delegate seating is assigned by state. I'm told every seat in the house is a great seat. However, Indiana's seat is not quite as great as, say, Massachusetts', Iowa's, Ohio's and North Carolina's.

And although we may not be considered to be indispensible to a victory in the fall, we are, however, directly in front of Hawaii's delegation and have a closer view of the podium than delegates from Guam and Samoa.

But at the end of the day–and I trust my fellow Samoan delegates would agree–just being there is all that really matters.

Tuesday–Since 1960, I've watched people on TV at national political conventions wearing funny hats, waving signs and applauding wildly at just about every statement from the podium. I've always wondered, "Who are these people?"

On Monday night, with the exception of the funny hat, I was one of "those people."

If you're looking for me on TV, I'm the one waving the sign, applauding wildly, but without the funny hat.

Wednesday–On my way into the arena, I saw former U.S. Attorney General Janet Reno, introduced myself and told her I was a prosecutor from Evansville, knowing that she was formerly the prosecutor of

Miami. She asked me about my views on exonerating defendants with DNA. I tried to say something intelligent. She told me about a North Carolina case in which the defendant was cleared because of DNA evidence, and that she was very interested in the subject. Then she actually asked me for my card so that she could contact me later and discuss the topic in more depth. I gave her the card.

Tuesday night's speakers were good, but most delegates agreed the previous night, with Gore, Carter and the Clintons, was an impossible act to follow. Sen. Ted Kennedy and Illinois' candidate for Senate, Barack Obama, were crowd favorites Tuesday.

I may have been the only one in the entire convention hall to applaud when Sen. Tom Daschle praised former deputy prosecutor John Kerry for "working hard to put criminals behind bars."

Thursday–Unlike the previous two evenings, when I stayed in the Indiana delegation seating area the entire time, Wednesday night I decided to explore the FleetCenter. I was surprised I was allowed to walk through the aisles and directly in front of the podium. From there, I could see the Teleprompter. Then I went to the upper-level floor, where the corporations had their VIP suites. My delegate pass allowed me access to most places in the arena, but not into the suites. However, walking up and down the hallways in front of the suites to watch the VIPs walk in and out is permitted. I did this for a while, and now for the name-dropping:

I walked by Spike Lee, Chris Wallace, Kwame and Omarosa from "The Apprentice," Fred Willard, Lewis Black, John Glenn and Katie Couric. The high point, or low point, came when I saw Larry David.

There is obviously an unwritten rule that you do not approach the celebrities in that area. In other parts of the arena, pictures, handshakes and autographs are commonplace. But if the chosen wanted to hang with you, they wouldn't be in a private suite to begin with.

For almost the entire time, I followed this rule. When I walked by Katie Couric, I pretended I didn't know who she was. When other celebrities walked by, I acted like I belonged there and was on my way to my own private suite.

But when I saw Larry David, star and writer of "Curb Your Enthusiasm," one of my favorite shows, instinct took over. I blurted out, "Larry David!" and stopped walking. He paused, instantly realized I was someone he didn't want to stop for, and said, "How ya doin'," barely breaking stride. Then I knew it was time to return to my seat.

Friday–If someone had told me a year ago that I would be at the FleetCenter in Boston, hear Carole King and Willie Nelson sing and John Kerry give a political speech, and that the speech would be far more exciting, I would have thought they (or I) were crazy.

But Thursday night that's exactly how it was for me and my other 4,400 or so delegates.

Celebrity obituary would make unusual reading

It seems that almost every celebrity who dies these days exits in scandal – Rock Hudson, Rick Nelson, and, recently, Len Bias.

It's so commonplace now, it might be more newsworthy if a death occurred under a different set of circumstances.

***

LOS ANGELES–Authorities are still sifting through clues in the wake of the timely and expected death of veteran movie star, Joe Celebrity.

The sheriff's department reportedly conducted a search of Celebrity's vehicle, and impounded an envelope found in the glove compartment containing no traces of cocaine.

A search of his residence also revealed no pills, no marijuana, and no drug paraphernalia.

In addition, a source close to the investigation said that a check of Celebrity's background revealed that Celebrity had been a closet monogamous heterosexual his 30 years of marriage. "Being a movie star, he tried to keep it a secret, but we have positive proof that Celebrity never had an affair with a fellow actress or actor his entire career," the source said.

Hollywood insiders, already grief stricken by the actor's death, were stunned by the double-barreled bombshell of Celebrity's drug and sex habits.

One of Celebrity's former director's said, "I never dreamed the guy didn't do coke. He seemed so vibrant. But when you think about it, that shouldn't make any difference in how he's remembered. As far as I'm concerned, not doing drugs shouldn't taint his image one iota."

Others were equally supportive. One actress who co-starred in several pictures with Celebrity said, "So he didn't mess around. Is that any reason to crucify the guy? I can't say I'm surprised though. When he used to tell me he couldn't have a drink with me because he had to go home to his wife, I began to suspect he was going home to his wife. I never asked him why. I'm sure he had his reasons. As long as it didn't affect his performance, I didn't think it was any of my business."

Celebrity's eldest daughter announced that none of his children would be writing a book about how badly they were treated. "Why should we? We all had a normal childhood," she said.

A police spokesman confirmed there was no evidence Celebrity mistreated his children. "Being in the limelight all those years affects different people in different ways. Apparently Celebrity handled the pressure by treating his children nicely, taking them to the zoo and ball games – things like that. Hey, it takes all kinds."

Celebrity's funeral is scheduled for tomorrow and the coroner still has not released the official cause of death. But since the most common causes of death – drug overdose, suicide, AIDS, cirrhosis of the liver, and murder have been eliminated, the official cause of death is expected to be listed as "natural causes."

There's a first time for everything.

Why when candidates smoke, there's no fire?

Evan Bayh, Democrat candidate for governor, called a news conference this week to announce he smoked marijuana 14 years ago while a freshman at Indiana University in Bloomington.

"I tried it; I didn't like it, and I never tried it again. It was a mistake I made when I was 18, one that I regret. I submitted in a moment of weakness to peer pressure."

Bayh said that his father was understanding when informed of the incident. Bayh hoped the voters also would understand.

I hate to pick on Evan, since he's just the most recent in a long line of distinguished office seekers – including presidential candidates and Supreme Court nominees – who has admitted to youthful drug transgressions. But before I draw any conclusions, there are a few questions I'd want answered.

Did all these confessors hire the same speechwriter? "It happened a long time ago...I only did it once or twice...I hated every second of it...I was very young at the time and I succumbed to peer pressure."

Bayh's confession is so similar to what Frank McCloskey said in his last campaign that it makes me wonder if they're talking about the same incident. They both happened in Bloomington in the early '70s.

(Wouldn't it be something if McCloskey was the peer who pressured Bayh? And if Bayh is elected governor, is smoking pot at

IU in the earlier '70s going to become a prerequisite for public office in Indiana?)

One thing that concerns me about all these confessions is that not one of these transgressors seemed to like it. Out of all those people, didn't anyone ever get high? Just one time during these misdeeds, didn't anyone ever put on a set of headphones and listen to "Sgt. Pepper"? Didn't anyone ever pass around some fudge brownies or Rocky Road ice cream?

And why is it that they always get talked into it in a moment of weakness? You'd think their leadership traits would have prompted at least one of them to ask to try it. And I find it amazing that no one seems to have tried it more than once or twice. Didn't anyone decide that the experiment needed four or five more tests before any valid conclusions could be drawn?

As for Bayh, I seriously doubt traces of the illegal substance are still remaining in his system. I don't worry that as a result of his transgression that his term of office as governor will be punctuated by getting the giggles during his State of the State addresses.

I'm not at all concerned about any uncontrollable urges to leave the governor's mansion in the early morning hours to cruise the streets of Indianapolis looking for an open convenience store in search of a box of Twinkies.

On the whole, I don't believe the admission did him any harm. Wouldn't it be interesting though, if the next office seeker who admits his transgressions says something like the following?

"When I was in college I occasionally smoked marijuana with friends. I did it often enough that I can't remember the exact number of times. We didn't think it was harmful and we didn't care if it was illegal. But we sure had some good times. I can see now that I was reckless, but if I had it to do all over again, I wouldn't change a thing."

Original members a good thing, but it's the act that lives on

The Temptations are advertising a concert at the Ford Center later this month. Maybe not The Temptations exactly, since of the original five members, only Otis Williams will be on stage.

But I suppose encouraging people to buy tickets to Twenty Per Cent of The Temptations wouldn't have the same appeal.

I go to a lot of these oldies concerts. Sometimes it's to see a portion of the original group that advertises itself as that group without qualification, like The Temptations. And sometimes it's a band with no original members that frequently names itself as a reference to the real band, such as The Fab Four, a Beatles tribute band.

These partially original bands and tribute bands can create some perplexing situations. Occasionally, it gets really bizarre, like when a fake Ace Frehley left his Kiss tribute band to replace the real Ace in Kiss. In that case, Tommy Thayer acted as Ace in the tribute band, but was himself in Kiss.

The question of how many members of the group can be missing before the band can no longer be reasonably referred to by its original name is a subjective one. For example, if Ringo decided to tour with three other musicians, no one would accept it as a Beatles concert, no matter how good they were.

Yet, I think it's different with The Temptations. I'd prefer more than one original member, but because they all dressed, danced and sounded alike and the fact that the other four originals have moved on to Rock and Roll Heaven, I can live with one out of five.

Ultimately, it's not the numbers, it's the act. If I go to New York to see The Rockettes, I'm not going to be a bit disappointed if I don't see a chorus of elderly women kicking up their heels. There's not a chance I'm going to think, "They were OK, but it wasn't the same as seeing the original Rockettes."

A play about a band can also create issues. I was in Las Vegas recently and attended a performance of "Jersey Boys," the story of The Four Seasons. During the play, there was a scene when the four actors playing the boys from Jersey had their backs to the real audience playing to an imaginary Las Vegas audience. It was surreal.

You had four talented singers who weren't really a band, but were pretending to be the Four Seasons, while they sang to an audience that wasn't there, while the real audience watched.

When the song was over, I didn't know whether to clap in character as if I were a member of that imaginary audience from decades ago or to clap as myself. Ultimately, my indecision resulted in my not being credible in either role.

So, am I going to be clapping as a real member of Temptations audience? It's a question I have yet to answer.

But I'm definitely tempted.

Provocative prosecutor will just lose on appeal

News item:

Brenda Taylor, 25, a prosecutor in Fort Lauderdale, Fla., faces dismissal from her job because, her boss said, her designer dresses are too provocative. She has filed a discrimination complaint against John Countryman, assistant state attorney. Countryman contends Ms. Taylor's skirts are too short and her style of dress "excites" defense attorneys.

I believe Ms. Taylor's boss made the right decision in showing her the door.

Trying a case against an excited defense attorney is like fighting a rabid dog. While the dog might be out of control, it's still a formidable opponent.

Trial folklore is filled with tales of provocatively dressed prosecutors who aroused their opponents into winning efforts.

I've found through the years of experience that the key to winning cases as a prosecutor is not to excite your opponent. A subdued defense attorney is a lot easier to handle than someone in the throes of a haberdashery-induced frenzy.

I like to think of the courtroom as a hospital. I'm the doctor and the defense attorney is the patient. My job is to keep the defense attorney subdued at all times.

But since I don't have the drugs to administer to the patient to keep him sedated like the medical profession has, I have to rely on the two most powerful tools of the legal profession to get the job done – trickery and deceit.

To the untrained observer, keeping a defense attorney quiet may seem like a difficult, if not impossible, task, but to the experienced attorney like yours truly, it's a piece of cake.

I try to speak in a quiet monotone at all times.

"Your honor, the defense attorney's scurrilous behavior is forensic misconduct at its worst," will hardly raise an eyebrow from your opponent if you say it soothingly.

Likewise, I'm very careful to make sure my chair doesn't squeak, I avoid rustling papers, and I never slam my briefcase on the table if the defense attorney is within earshot.

I intentionally wear non-provocative clothes with bland colors. While my natural instinct may be to the flashy provocative, I make it a point to wear subdued browns and blues.

I know some people think the reason I keep wearing the same suits and ties to court is because I don't have an extensive wardrobe, but actually it's a strategic move on my part so that my opponents will get used to what I'm wearing.

If I've done my job properly, by the time of final argument, the defense attorney will be so bored he'll be unable to summon the proper emotion to sway the jury to his side.

Perhaps Ms. Taylor has a reason for dressing provocatively. But I say, let sleeping defense attorneys lie.

Compulsive gambler is a Rose by another name

America wants to know: Is Pete Rose a compulsive gambler?

In an interview in a recent Sports Illustrated, Rose said no. Of course, this is the same guy who said, "If I were a betting man, I'd bet I never bet on any baseball games."

I don't know enough about Rose to offer an opinion on whether he's a compulsive gambler. But I've been to a racetrack more than once or twice and have been around gambling enough to know how to spot a compulsive gambler.

***

If you make more than one bet every three months on the weather.

If you have so many bets going you have to write them down.

If you're more interested in the point spread than the result of the game.

If you know that vigorish has nothing to do with energy.

If you're expressing a thought and you say "I bet" more often than "I think."

If you ask what time it is and someone says it's 5 to 1, you immediately think it'll pay $12 to win.

If someone talks about jumping into a pool and you reach for your wallet.

If you attend a business seminar in Las Vegas and claim that you went there for business purposes.

If you don't think of cigars when you hear Amarillo Slim.

If someone says jockey shorts and you picture Willie Shoemaker's underwear and not Jim Palmer.

If you bet against your favorite team because of the point spread.

If your favorite team is really who covers the spread most often.

If you see a car license plate that reads – 82-288 and you think, "Full house."

If you ever go to the track and hope you break even because you need the money.

If you think racehorses are great athletes.

If you go to a county fair that has pig racing and you bet on which pig will win.

If over half of the above situations describe you, then I'd bet, if I were a betting man, that you may be a compulsive gambler.

Boston Marathon was a milestone - mile for mile

In 1985, Bob Gaudet, an old college friend, and I made a pact to run the 1986 Boston Marathon. We didn't do it.

In 1986, we vowed to run the 1987 Boston Marathon. We didn't do it.

In 1987, we vowed to run the 1988 Boston Marathon. Monday we did it.

To qualify for Boston, I'd have to run a marathon under 3 hours, 10 minutes. Although I'm a veteran of three marathons, having finished last twice and not last once, my previous best time for the 26.2 miles was slightly more than an hour and a half slower than the qualifying minimum.

Another way to qualify is to be a doctor. While I am a doctor of jurisprudence, apparently that doesn't count. It seems discriminatory that slow-running doctors are allowed to enter while slow-running lawyers have to resort to extralegal means to fulfill their fantasies.

I suppose they allow doctors to run so that in case a runner needs medical attention, there'll be plenty of doctors available on the course. I think lawyers would be far more useful.

Suppose you were hit by a car during the run and suffered a personal injury; who would you rather have running next to you – a good doctor or a good lawyer?

Remember when Rosie Ruiz cheated and supposedly came in first in the 1980 women's marathon? It took marathon officials about an hour before they disqualified her. A good lawyer would have slapped an injunction on her before she crossed the finish line.

And wouldn't a lawyer be a lot more useful than a doctor to a world-class marathoner who needs to negotiate a lucrative shoe contract?

Realizing my chances of persuading the Boston Athletic Association to allow lawyers to qualify was about the same as my running a 3:10 marathon or graduating medical school, I decided to run the race "unofficially."

While unofficial runners are welcome, you don't get a number, you have to start behind the other 6,700 runners, but most importantly, no race official will record your finish for posterity or give you a medal when you cross the line.

I began the race wearing a trash bag, hoping to keep dry until the rain stopped. It took five minutes to reach the starting line and I discarded the bag soon after, although it rained practically the whole race.

What I didn't realize is that in the Boston Marathon you are what you wear. Many runners wore shirts with simple bold messages such as their name or alma mater, and the crowd cheered them on accordingly.

Gaudet wore a Boston Red Sox T-shirt and all along the route was exhorted by shouts of "Go Red Sox." I, on the other hand, wore a shirt that read, "Old National Bank; West Side Nut Club Fall Festival; Road Races."

The print was so small and the crowd of runners so large that at first the spectators couldn't read it, so I received no personal encouragement.

As the race progressed and the runners thinned out and I slowed down, making my message easier to read, the crowd began to urge me on with shouts of "Hang in there Old National Bank," and "You're looking good Old National."

It was a very strange feeling to have my entire identity in the Boston Marathon wrapped up in an Old National Bank T-shirt. Still, as I thought about how I began the race, it was a whole lot better than having people yell, "You're looking good, trash bag."

The cheering crowds were fantastic, but the highlight was at Wellesley College, about the 12-mile point. Hundreds of coeds lined the street in a non-stop screaming frenzy, and for a few glorious moments I knew what it was like to be Bruce Springsteen.

I reached the halfway point at 2:08:41, a full two seconds before Ibrahim Hussein won the race, but for me it was all uphill from there.

I'd hoped to run to the hills, about Mile 17.5, without stopping, but I ran out of gas just after Mile 15. By the time I got to Heartbreak Hill, my heart was already broken and many other parts of my anatomy were fading fast.

I walked, jogged and shuffled the last 11 miles. I wanted to finish in under five hours, and I sort of did. I crossed the line five hours and one minute after the race officially began, but since it took me five minutes to get to the starting line and since I didn't run officially, I guess I can say I finished in under five hours.

Gaudet, running in his first race, spurred on by the "Go Red Sox" cheers, blazed the distance in 4:09, in plenty of time to capture my finish for posterity, even if the Boston Athletic Association doesn't recognize it.

I'm tempted to call it a once-in-a-lifetime experience, but Gaudet and I are already talking about 1989.

After this, things never look the same

And now Boston, and not just Boston. The Boston Marathon.

This one hits too close to home, mainly because Boston is my first home, having been born, graduated high school and indoctrinated as a lifelong Red Sox fan there.

A mere 50 years ago, as a high school junior who got the day off because of Patriot's Day, I stood at Beacon Street less than a mile from our apartment and watched the runners head toward Boylston Street only two miles from the finish line. Right in front of me, Aurele Vandendressche, the eventual winner, passed the great Abebe Bikila, barefoot and fading, for what was to be Bikila's only defeat in 15 marathon attempts. At that time there were about 200 runners, not the more than 20,000 of today.

If someone asked me that day what I thought the chances of my ever running the Boston Marathon were, I would have acknowledged it was possible, but exceptionally unlikely. Had they continued asking what I thought the chances were that someday someone would detonate bombs at the finish line, I probably wouldn't have understood the question.

Seven months later, President John F. Kennedy was assassinated, and for me, the world was never the same. When Kennedy was killed, I was disoriented. It made no sense. I had trouble believing it at first, because it was an event unlike anything I'd ever experienced.

But since then, I react differently to tragedy, no matter how horrific. The World Trade Center. Mass murders in a movie theater. Slaughtering of schoolchildren. I never again say, "I don't believe it. This can't be happening." I'm not matter of fact about it, but I accept it immediately and wonder what's next.

And one thing's for sure, something will be next.

Twenty five years after watching that marathon and becoming a recreational runner, I actually ran in the Boston Marathon. I didn't qualify, as real runners do, but in those days, about half the runners were "bandits," which was acceptable to both organizers and spectators, as long as you started at the back.

I started at the back and finished in the back in 5 hours, a time that embarrassed me, but one I would be overjoyed to be able to run today. When I got to the finish, I'm certain I felt like I was going to die. I'm also certain it didn't cross my mind that I might get blown up. I'm planning on running the Indianapolis Half Marathon in two weeks. Since I haven't been able to run for more than a month, if I do it, it will be way more of a struggle than normal, and I'm sure as I near the finish, I'll feel like I'm going to die — not literally.

But this time, something will be different. Still being a probability guy, I won't be worried about it, but I'm certain it will cross my mind. It's theoretically possible I could be blown up now.

The world has changed more than a little since that April afternoon in 1963.

CHAPTER

5

Actor did it his way - in a gorilla costume

Actor did it his way - in a gorilla costume

I like reading the interesting facts in the biographies about the actors in the programs that are handed out at local theater productions. They generally include the actor or actress's hometown, educational background and prior acting experience.

Often when their acting experience is limited, you can count on something like, "Christine is delighted to be in the ensemble and wants to thank her parents for all their support." Most of the time, the biographies are more detailed.

I recently attended a production of "Death of a Salesman." The program contained its usual summaries of hometowns, colleges, relatives and prior acting experience, but I was most intrigued by the bio of J.S.M., the actor playing Willy Loman.

J.S.M. was a member of the Screen Actors Guild and his "big break came when he was cast as a gorilla in the film "Gorillas in the Mist." He also wore a gorilla suit opposite Frank Sinatra for an international commercial campaign."

When the curtain went up, I couldn't concentrate on the dialogue. I was wondering if, when J.S.M. first applied for membership in the SAG, did he imagine his credits would one day include playing opposite Frank Sinatra in a gorilla suit? And if so, how would he have felt about it?

HE'S A MAN WAY OUT THERE IN THE BLUE, RIDING ON A SMILE AND A SHOESHINE.

Frank had a reputation as a demanding taskmaster. Did he see J.S.M. in "Gorillas in the Mist" and was so impressed with the performance that he demanded, "Get me that gorilla who was to the left of Sigourney Weaver near the big rock." Or did J.S.M. simply get the job because he was the only one who wasn't deterred by the ad which read, "No one without prior gorilla experience need apply."

NOTHING'S PLANTED. I DON'T HAVE A THING IN THE GROUND.

Are other actors awed by his prior co-starring with Sinatra or do they make fun of him behind his back? And should you be especially concerned about making fun of someone who has shown himself capable of acting like a gorilla?

ATTENTION MUST BE PAID.

But sadly, I couldn't pay attention like I should have. He was not a believable Willy Loman. I just couldn't get the image out of my mind of Frank Sinatra singing "My Way," while a hairy J.S.M. interrupted the song with gorilla-like grunts.

He probably would have been better off it just said, "J.S.M. is delighted to be appearing in the lead role as Willy Loman and wants to thank his parents for all their support."

Some girls drive dads to nervous breakdown

Mick Jagger's 16-year-old daughter, Jade, has been kicked out of her boarding school for breaking curfew to date her boyfriend. The elder Jagger had reportedly warned her to stay away from the boy.

It's hard to imagine Mick with a teen-age daughter. I can only guess what the conversation is like after Jade's boyfriend goes to the Jagger residence to pick up Jade for a date.

***

"I wonder why he wants us back so early, Jade."

"My dad's like that. He's afraid if I stay out late, I'll get in trouble."

"How much trouble could a 16-year-old girl get into in London in just one night? It's not like I'm a murderer or something."

"I know. I told him that. But he says he remembers when he was your age. You wouldn't believe what I had to go through just to get him to agree to let me go on this date."

"Hey, I still think your dad's pretty neat. What does he do?"

"I don't know. He says he's in the world's greatest rock 'n' roll band."

"You mean Whitesnake?"

"No, the Rolling Stones or something. They used to be big a long time ago."

"What instrument did he play?"

126

"He didn't actually plan an instrument. He'd take off his shirt, wear tight pants and run around the stage, I guess. He says the girls thought he was real sexy."

"You're kidding. Him?"

"Yeah. I know. It's hard to believe. But this was a long time ago."

"What's it like having a dad like that?"

"It's OK, except sometimes he embarrasses me. Like when I introduced you to him and he did a backflip and said, 'Pleased to meet you and I hope you guess my name.' He's always doing stuff like that. I guess he thinks he's funny."

"Hey, don't worry about it. I thought it was cool."

"I guess it's hard for him to let go of the past."

"My parents are like that too. What a drag it must be getting old."

'Literally' had to write this column

I've been trying a murder case for the past seven weeks, which is a pretty good excuse for not writing any columns.

I hadn't intended to write again, if at all, until the trial was over, which probably won't be for more than a month.

But something's been bothering me, and I need to get it off my chest, not literally.

I can't stop saying the word "literally."

Well, not literally, because if that were true, all I would do for 24 hours a day is say "literally." And even then, it might not be because I couldn't stop but because I chose not to stop, since it could be by choice and not compulsion. Although why anyone would choose to say "literally" nonstop is literally beyond my comprehension.

Perhaps it would be more accurate to say, I've become aware that I overuse the word "literally" and I'm trying to reduce the frequency, but it's been difficult.

It all began about a month ago when I was watching The Colbert Report. Stephen Colbert said that some dictionary has added a new definition to the word "literally." Since people so commonly misuse the word (e.g. When someone says, 'The speech was so boring, I thought it was literally never going to end,' they don't really mean they didn't think the speech would end, but used the word "literally" to emphasize how long the speech went on.), the dictionary has added an alternate meaning to include the way people use it incorrectly, for emphasis, even if it's not literally true.

As Colbert pointed out, "literally" can now mean, "not literally."

The next morning, the defense attorney in my trial told the jurors that they "literally had the defendant's life in their hands." Having just watched The Colbert Report and being a former English teacher, I objected to his use of the word.

I don't mean to minimize the seriousness of the jurors' duty, because it's true, the defendant's future freedom may depend on their verdict. But unless he was on the other side of a cliff and the only thing that was preventing a lethal fall was his holding on to a juror's hand, then it would be incorrect to say they "literally" held his life in their hands.

Since then, I began to notice how often I use the word "literally." I don't make the mistake of substituting it when I mean "figuratively," but apparently I've been saying it way too often – and before Colbert, I literally never noticed it.

It's not just me saying it too much that bothers me. I've become painfully aware that other people overuse it. Now when someone says "literally," even correctly, it sticks out like a sore thumb, not literally, but figuratively.

Has our ability to express ourselves deteriorated to the point where we can't be believed unless we emphasize our thought with "literally"?

It looks like about another five weeks of trial ahead and all I know is I literally don't have time to think about this anymore.

One man out of baseball movie may put fix in for grandkids

"Eight Men Out," a movie about the 1919 World Series fix, will be coming soon to a theater near you. Faithful readers will no doubt remember the column I wrote last fall about my part in the film.

For the unfaithful, a brief review is in order: John Dempsey, a friend of mine from Boston, is a friend of the director, John Sayles. When Dempsey heard they were looking for extras to play the World Series crowd, he called me and we met at the film location in Indianapolis for our chance at celluloid immortality.

The overcast day, which limited the extras who showed up, and Dempsey's connections allowed us to be involved in practically every crowd scene.

But the piece de resistance was when Dempsey and I were placed right behind Christopher Lloyd for a couple of crucial scenes.

When we finished the day's filming, I knew there was no way we were not going to be in this movie. The only question was whether or not we'd appeared in enough scenes for a "best supporting actor" nomination.

Soon after filming was completed, Doug Brown joined the prosecutor's office. Doug had worked on the entire movie as a driver for the cast and was also in a number of crowd scenes since he was on the set every day.

Very few days went by from the time Doug joined the staff until two weeks ago that Doug and I didn't talk about our impending movie debut.

Winter and spring came and went and the thought of being on the silver screen, larger than life, got me through some bleak winter days.

It's hard to explain why this was so important. I just had this vision of my great-grandchildren sitting in front of some TV set saying to their little friends with pride, "That's my great-granddaddy sitting behind Christopher Lloyd."

Two weeks ago I got a call from Doug, inviting me to go to Chicago for the movie's worldwide debut. I couldn't go, but I told him where to look for me.

"I'll probably be in about a dozen scenes, but there's one where I'm right behind Christopher Lloyd and his gambling friend says to him, 'You think you can stake me to train fare back to Philly?'"

The next morning I waited with eager anticipation to find out which scenes I was in.

"I looked for you, Stan, but I didn't see you," Doug said.

"That's impossible. I was right there. Maybe they cut the scene about train fare back to Philly."

"No, that was in it, but I didn't see you. Maybe I wasn't looking in the right place."

"Were you in it?" I asked.

"Yeah, there's this one scene at the end where Charlie Sheen's talking about throwing the Series and I'm right there listening."

"Hey, that's great Doug," I said, trying to be gracious, but all I could think of was his great-grandchildren laughing at my great-grandchildren.

I walked away shaking my head. There had to be some logical explanation, but the only one I could come up with was that I was so convincing acting like a 1919 spectator that Doug didn't recognize the 1988 me.

I was troubled enough to call Dempsey that evening.

"John, there's this guy in my office who saw 'Eight Men Out,' and I know this is ridiculous, but he…"

"We're not in it, Stanley."

"What do you mean we're not in it? We've got to be in it. We were right there behind Christopher Lloyd."

"I talked to Sayles at a wedding a couple of weeks ago. Remember how cloudy it was the day we were there? They had to throw out all the scenes they shot that day and reshoot them."

"Say it ain't so, John."

"I'm sorry."

"Why didn't you call me when you found out?"

"I knew how much this meant to you. I couldn't bring myself to tell you."

"C'mon. What's the big deal? I'm an adult. Who cares if we're in some dumb movie?"

That was two weeks ago. And every time I see an interview about the movie or read another review, it hurts. I keep telling myself, "It's only a movie. It's only a movie," but that doesn't seem to help much.

I suppose that someday I'll get over it, but I can't help but wonder if my great-grandchildren ever will.

Wimps...Hard to define, but easy to recognize

Wimps are getting a bad name these days.

Not too long ago, politicians held press conferences to assert they were not crooks. But I was in New York last week and governor Cuomo announced in a press conference that his mild-mannered running-mate was definitely not a wimp.

According to George Will, who looks like a wimp, George Bush will not get elected President because he's a wimp. Bush's reaction, the quintessential wimp response, was that he still had a lot of respect for Will.

I've got a dictionary about five inches thick, with over 320,000 words, but "wimp" is not among them. Still it's one of those words whose meaning is evident the first time you hear it in a sentence. I don't recall the first time I heard someone say, "What a wimp," but I'm certain I knew what it meant.

The difficulty in defining the word is not unlike the dilemma that Justice Potter Stewart had with obscenity – I know it when I see it.

Wimpdom is not confined to one political party. Nixon may have been a crook, but he wasn't a wimp. Mondale was, Humphrey was, but Kennedy and Johnson weren't. Truman looked like one, but wasn't. Goldwater wasn't, but Eisenhower and Ford would have been if it hadn't been for war and football, two activities anathema to wimps.

Today anti-wimp fervor has gotten out of hand, particularly since Reagan, who is definitely not one, beat Carter, the only indisputable wimp-president of the second-half of the 20th Century.

I don't know if I am one, although I suspect that anyone who doesn't know for sure probably is. But, in any event, the time has come to be kind to wimps. They possess qualities that should be encouraged rather than castigated. They're meek, eager to please, soft-spoken, and polite.

If I had my choice, I'd rather have the next generation grow up to be more like Alan Alda than Sylvester Stallone.

But if the present trend continues, pretty soon there won't be any wimps left. And then there won't be anybody for non-wimps to push around. It could spell disaster for our country.

So if you know a wimp, do something nice for him this week. Compliment him on his tie or jazz collection. Or better still, take a wimp to lunch.

You'll feel better and so will the wimp.

By any other name
she'd be as sweet

Many years ago Susie and I acquired a nameless black kitten. I named it "Reno," a name that suited this feline more appropriately than any other combination of letters in the universe.

When a bank held a contest to name its new automatic teller, I entered "Tallulah Bank." It didn't win, but I attribute that to the judges' lack of wisdom rather than the quality of the entry.

But for some reason, when it comes to naming my own children, my creative juices stop flowing. This week I had another opportunity.

The baby, a girl, arrived on schedule. Since this wasn't a total surprise, you'd think I would have been better prepared, but I kept thinking inspiration would strike.

We'd been discussing names for months, but the only thing Susie and I could agree on was that I didn't like any of her suggestions and she didn't like any of mine.

When the little bundle of joy arrived on Monday, we were no closer to naming her than we were nine months ago. So we started from scratch.

"How about Brittany, Tiffany or Crystal?" she said.

"No. Too trendy. I don't want her having a bunch of other kids in class with the same name. What about Amity, Felicity or Charity?" I countered.

"You're kidding, right?"

"Not really. But maybe those names are a little much."

"How about Michelle or Renee?"

"Too French," I said.

"What about Christina or Christine?"

"Too Christian."

By Tuesday morning we had made no progress, so we went through the name books, birth announcements, marriage licenses and obituaries. We even began getting friends involved.

By Tuesday night, with Susie's discharge from the hospital scheduled for the following morning, we still hadn't chosen a name, but a least we had narrowed it down to Jeanine or Caroline.

I got a call from Susie Wednesday morning. "It's going to be Jeanine."

"What about sweet Caroline, good times never seemed so good."

"Sorry. It's Jeanine. The hospital invoked the 'J' rule. It's out of our hands."

"The 'J' rule? I never heard of that."

"I didn't either until this morning. But there's a rule that if you still haven't picked a name on the day you're going to be discharged, then you must pick a name beginning with the letter 'J'. It's in the small print on the waiver I signed when I was admitted."

"So that explains why so many boys are named Jason, Jonathan or Joshua and all the girls are either Jennifer, Jessica…"

"Or Jeanine."

"Or Jeanine," I sighed.

"I hope you're not too disappointed."

"I guess not. I always preferred Cracklin' Rosie to Sweet Caroline anyway."

Even turban-powered ayatollah stalls at times

Editor's note: The Evansville Courier does not condone the following blasphemous article about the Ayatollah Khomeini. We recognize this article is in extremely poor taste and an affront to all those who worship Khomeini. All death threats and any other forms of reprisal should be directed to the author. We do request that if any reward is offered, it be at least $5.2 million.

In a speech this week commemorating the beginning of the Persian New Year, the Ayatollah Khomeini urged Moslems to overcome their carnal desires, but confessed to be unable to control himself.

"In his lifetime, man is afflicted with carnal desires. He needs self-discipline and I, as the speaker of these words, have not succeeded in this task," the ayatollah said.

I always thought of the ayatollah as a wild and crazy guy, but until he confessed his lack of self-discipline, I never pictured him as a soldier in the carnal battlefields. But I suppose he's just a guy like the rest of us, who puts on his sandals one foot at a time.

If the ayatollah went to a bar, except for his turban and robes, he'd probably be indistinguishable from every guy in the place.

***

137

"Hi. My name's Ayatollah Khomeini. Can I buy you a drink?"

"Sure. I'll have what you're having."

"Bartender. Two mineral waters here, please."

"Mineral water? Are you on the wagon?"

"Not really. Drinking is against my religion."

"Hey, you're funny. What did you say your name was?"

"Ayatollah Khomeini, but my friends call me A.K."

"Do you come here often, A.K.?"

"Not too often. I get lonely sometimes. I have trouble meeting girls."

"A good-looking guy like you? Have you tried church socials?"

"Sure. But it seems like all the good ones are married."

"Ain't that the truth. Have you ever tried it?"

"Well, I've outlived two wives. My first marriage was in 1928."

"Gosh. How old are you?"

"I'm 88."

"No kidding. I wouldn't have guessed over 62. I think the beard and turban make you look younger."

"I try to keep in shape. I find that putting in a full day at work tends to keep me young."

"It's remarkable that a man of your age is still working. What line of work are you in?"

"Oh, this and that. Executions, proclamations, edicts…stuff like that."

"Do you like music, A.K.?"

"Sure, Cat Stevens is one of my favorites. You know, 'Morning has broken.'"

"Oh yeah, I've heard of him. But that was 20 years ago, wasn't it?"

"I guess I'm a traditional kind of guy."

"What about books?"

"I don't like the best sellers. Give me the Koran any day. Say, would you like to come up to my apartment and read the Koran with me?"

"It's getting late. I've gotta go."

"Hey, wait a minute. Did anyone ever tell you you'd look awfully cute in a veil?"

Yankees' Tommy John's departure dashed diamond dreams

Last week, the New York Yankees released Tommy John, thereby dashing my dreams of ever becoming a major-league baseball player.

John, at age 46, was the oldest active big-league ballplayer and, as of Tuesday, for the first time in my life, there are no major-league ballplayers older than I am.

When I say my dreams were dashed, I guess I need to explain.

There are dreams and there are dreams. Some dreams, which I'll call Class C dreams, really can come true. If you work hard enough or are in the right place at the right time, they could happen. It's not beyond belief to find the girl of your dreams or land the job of your dreams.

Then you have your Class B dreams. They're the ones that might come true, but probably won't. For example, people win the lottery every day. You might be one of those people, but you probably won't be.

Finally, there are Class A dreams, ones that you know won't come true, but they're theoretically possible. However, in order to have a legitimate Class A dream, there must be some basis in reality. For instance, you might dream about being President of the United States, but dreaming about being King of Saturn would not be appropriate.

Playing major-league ball was my Class A dream, and until Tuesday, my basis in reality was that as long as there was someone older than I am still playing, it was theoretically possible.

Even before this week, my dream of the major league has never been anything more than a theoretical possibility. Ever since I failed to make the Little Leagues, I've known my career wasn't destined to be on the diamond, but that never stopped me from fantasizing about it.

I've played other sports, none really well, but almost all with more ability than baseball.

Despite playing tennis regularly over the years, I've never dreamed of winning Wimbledon. I've run in the Boston Marathon and finished less than three hours behind the winner, but never given a thought to wondering what it would be like to break the tape. I almost made my junior high basketball team, but I've never fantasized about going one-on-one with Michael Jordan.

But there's something special about baseball. It was the first adult game I played. It produced my first hero–Ted Williams. And I still dream about baseball cards – mostly 1954 Topps.

I'd much rather perfectly play the carom off the Green Monster at Fenway and hold the runner to a single than serve an ace to win a crucial set.

But with the departure of John, I'm no longer entitled to hang on to my dream. Just like being King of Saturn, it would violate the order of the universe as we know it.

I could practice every day. I could have expert coaches teach me how to hit, run and throw. I could take steroids.

But even if I became the very best 43-year-old baseball player in the world, I'd still be too old.

The only chance I have left, and I'll admit, it's a slim one, is for satanic intervention.

In the play "Damn Yankees," the devil tried to make a deal with Joe Hardy. The devil was offering major-league baseball career, not to mention Lola, in exchange for Hardy's eternal soul.

Even with Tommy John out of the picture, I suppose it's still possible I'll get the same offer. But I'm not going to get my hopes up.

After unscented soap, what's left to wish for?

"If the one thing you've always wished for was an unscented beauty bar, you've got two wishes left."

That's how a TV commercial is selling a brand of soap – I mean beauty bar.

Are there really people out there whose one wish is for an unscented beauty bar? If so, wouldn't it be a travesty to waste two more wishes on people like that?

"Let's see, Gary. If I had three wishes? That's a tough one. OK. First would definitely be an unscented beauty bar. Then. Oh, I don't know. Maybe a dripless deodorant and an autographed picture of Bert Convy."

***

Speaking of TV commercials, it pains me to watch Linda Ellerbee hawking coffee. She spent a career convincing us she wouldn't sell out. I guess before now no one offered her the right price.

***

I hear Chris Berman, with accompanying tennis videotape, say this on ESPN last Sunday. "Here she forces Sabatini into an unforced error."

I couldn't believe my ears. He should have said, 'Here, she unforces Sabatini into a forced error.'

***

There are Operation City Beautiful signs in Evansville which read: "Put litter in its place."

At first this seems like a noble sentiment. But actually litter that is strewn around streets and yards *is* in its place.

In order to qualify as litter, paper has to be out of place. If you picked it up and put it in the trash can, it would no longer be litter.

***

Rick Pitino, new Kentucky basketball coach vowed to "win right away," and then explained what he meant by that pledge.

"Whether that means in terms of wins and losses that show up, I'm not sure. I think that supporters of Kentucky basketball, forgetting the score, will leave the arena thinking that the basketball team is a winner."

Call me naive, but to me winning in basketball is when you score more points than the other side. I suppose I could agree that Kentucky's basketball team can still be winners, even if they lose, but only if they give at least 110 percent.

***

Bill Wyman, Rolling Stones' guitarist, at 52 is marrying Mandy Smith, 19, after a six-year courtship. Wyman's 28-year-old son is dating Mandy's 38-year-old mother. Trying to figure out the relationships at a Wyman family reunion reminds me of a math problem on the SATs.

Let's see. If Bill's son marries Mandy's mother, then Bill's son would be Mandy's stepfather and stepson. If Mandy's mother gives birth to a girl, that girl would be Bill's granddaughter and sister-in-law.

It all seemed so much simpler in the days when the only problem was not getting enough satisfaction.

***

Recently, the John F. Kennedy Profile in Courage Award was created to honor the slain president.

An Associated Press report covering the ceremony reported it thusly: After Sen. Edward Kennedy's remarks, reporters called on Mrs. Jacqueline Onassis, wearing a hot pink jacket and a black miniskirt.

After all these years, can't we describe Kennedy's widow without a fashion statement?

He did not seek, nor gracefully accept, puzzle gift

I was born on Father's Day.

According to family legend, my mother presented my father with his newborn son and offered, "This is your Father's Day present."

My father responded, "I was hoping for a tie."

I believe I inherited my inability to gracefully accept a gift from my father, may he rest in peace. I know it's supposed to be better to give than receive, but it doesn't really matter, since I'm not particularly good at either.

When it's time to give presents, if I don't delegate that chore to my wife, there's a good chance there will either be no present or, at best, an inappropriate one. In junior high school, I tried out for and was rejected for the part of Scrooge in our Christmas play, possibly because it seemed too much like typecasting, or maybe because they were looking for someone with a more positive attitude about gift giving.

As for gift receiving, I haven't improved much upon my father's Father's Day birthday example. It's not that I'm totally against the concept of receiving gifts. It's just that too often the gift causes me more anxiety than pleasure.

Take the most recent examples, which took place in the past few weeks. In an amazing coincidence, both my daughter and sister bought me jigsaw puzzles as a gift for my upcoming birthday.

I knew immediately I had no interest in doing either. Since it's the thought that counts, I would have preferred they just told me they were thinking of buying me a puzzle.

To be fair to them, I do occasionally like to put together a good jigsaw puzzle. My office walls are covered with about 20 framed puzzles, but they are all puzzles that I personally selected – mostly things like Beatles' album covers or baseball cards.

I didn't have the slightest desire to complete the gift puzzles of some too-clever mystery or some multi-sided thing that would likely require a degree in quantum physics to even attempt.

A puzzle is personal. If they bought me a tie or a shirt I didn't like, I'd have no problem wearing it once or twice.

But completing a puzzle involves a much greater commitment than simply putting on an article of clothing. It requires many hours of intense concentration. If you don't care about the finished product, that means many hours of intense misery.

There was no realistic chance I was going to do these puzzles, so what's the problem? I'm not any worse off than before I got them, right?

Au contraire. I now have to figure out how to inform my daughter and sister that I have no intention of ever using their carefully selected gift.

Tact is not generally my strong suit. I'd like to blame my father for that one too, but I think I may have acquired this trait on my own.

My natural inclination would be to say, "I don't have the slightest intentions of doing this puzzle. Why would you presume to choose a puzzle topic for me?" Although this may be natural, I don't say this because I realize it might be a little harsh.

On the other hand, if I say, "What a great idea. It's exactly what I wanted," someday I'm going to have to explain why I never opened the box.

I struggled with how to strike the right balance between totally rejecting their gift without hurting their feelings. Eventually, I came up with some lame explanation about how it was a very thoughtful and creative gift but I was just too busy at this time to give it the attention it deserved. If I hurt their feelings, they were both too tactful to say so.

I got by with it this time, and I'm home free—until the next time someone gives me a present I won't know how to gracefully accept.

So on this Father's Day, to all you fathers out there: may you all get the tie you wanted and if not, at least be able to act like you did anyway.

High times in some Super Bowl comments

The biggest things in Colorado these days are the Denver Broncos and legalized marijuana. The state of Washington, home of the Seattle Seahawks, already legalized pot back in 2010.

Who knows, now that it's legal in their home states, maybe the announcers and players sampled some of the product before today's big game. If so, I'm guessing the telecast of the Super Bowl will be a little different from what we're used to.

PREGAME INTERVIEW

Erin: I'm on the field with Peyton Manning before the game. Peyton, what kind of preparation have you done to take apart this Seattle defense?

Peyton: Preparation? You know, Erin, I think preparation is way overrated. The most important thing for me is to be relaxed. I do what I have to do to get relaxed, play a few of my favorite jazz cuts, think about the meaning of life and put on my uniform. And now I'm ready for whatever comes my way. We'll win if we're meant to win and if not, what's the big deal? They play it again next year, right?

Erin: What about the cold weather, Peyton? It's a 5 degree wind chill out there. Do you think it'll bother you?

147

Peyton: Five degrees, huh? I didn't notice. It won't bother me, but if I throw a Pick-Six, I'll just groove on the symmetry of the D-back running it in for a touchdown. You know, Erin, there aren't many sights more beautiful in football than a speedy defensive back gliding in for a score.

GAME COMMENTARY

Joe: It's third and long for Seattle. They need to convert this one. I'm Joe Buck, broadcasting this game for you with my partner Troy Aikman, who is still not here…Wait a minute, here comes Troy, now.

Troy: Sorry, man. I guess I just forgot. I'm at home watching the pregame ceremony and I hear them say my name as one of the announcers and I think, 'Oh, (bleep), I knew I was supposed to be somewhere this afternoon.'

Joe: Hey, don't sweat it, man. No big deal. It's not as if it changes the score.

Troy: What is the score anyways?

Joe: Don't know. Don't care. In the great scheme of things, what difference does it make, anyway? Say, have you ever noticed how orange the Broncos' uniforms are?

POSTGAME INTERVIEWS

Chris: I'm with Richard Sherman, who intercepted the great Peyton Manning twice. Richard, I guess this proves what you've been saying the past two weeks about Manning being a choke artist, right?

Richard: Did I say that? I don't remember. If I did, I didn't mean it. I just got lucky. Peyton Manning is a beautiful man. Hey, maybe that's why the first three letters of his last name are M, A, N. I never thought of that before.

Erin: Russell Wilson, you've just been selected MVP of the Super Bowl. Are you going to Disneyland?

Russell: No, Erin. I'm headed straight to my favorite buffet. I was so hungry out there during the final drive, the pigskin was starting to look like a giant juicy ham. And after the buffet, I'm taking my family out to eat.

A fair and impartial juror

I've been selected for the upcoming jury pool.

I realize my chances of actually serving on the jury are about the same as President Obama's selecting Sarah Palin as his running mate for 2012. However, that doesn't absolve me of playing the game and filling out my questionnaire completely and honestly.

There were 29 questions. I breezed through all of them other than Question #27, which asked, "Do you know of any valid reason that would disqualify you from jury service or why you could not serve as a fair and impartial juror?"

Hmmm. My fairness and impartiality have certainly been questioned by others, but is that a valid reason for disqualification. I know some defense attorneys who may think so.

***

Do you realize, Mr. Levco, the fact that a charge has been filed against my client raises no presumption of his guilt?

Sure, I realize that. I also realize that a charge couldn't have been filed unless a neutral and detached magistrate determined there was probable cause to believe your client was guilty. But even knowing that, I can set that aside and not consider it in my deliberations.

***

And if we choose to do so, we could present no evidence, not question a single witness and make no statement to the jury. How would you feel about that?

If you did that, I'd think you were an idiot or deliberately trying to set up grounds for appeal. I know there's no way you'll do nothing and if you did, it would get reversed in a heartbeat on appeal for ineffective assistance of counsel. But, bottom line, if you really did nothing and the case isn't proven, I'd have no problem with a not guilty verdict.

***

You don't believe the fact that a charge has been filed means my client is guilty, do you?

No. I think that would only be true well over 90% of the time. But hey, each case is different and even though I know it's highly likely your client is guilty, I realize it's possible he may not be or more probable that it can't be proven beyond a reasonable doubt, so I'll judge this case on its individual merits.

***

If my client chooses not to take the witness stand, would that set off any bells in your mind?

Ding. Ding. Ding. Of course it would. If he didn't do it, why not say so? I know, you'll have all kinds of explanations about why an innocent person would keep quiet when he's being accused, and I suppose there are theoretical legitimate strategy reasons to believe that not testifying makes him look less guilty. It's just that I've never personally encountered one. However, these days, I know most attorneys prefer to keep their client off the stand. Do I think it's an indicator of guilt? Absolutely. Will I hold that

151

against him or comment upon it in my deliberations after being instructed not to? Absolutely not.

***

After giving it appropriate consideration, I decided I might not be the ideal juror by some defense attorney standards, but I don't believe there are any "valid reasons that would disqualify me from jury service or why I couldn't serve as a fair and impartial juror," so I answered Question #27 accordingly and sent in my completed questionnaire and waited for the call. That was over a month ago and I still have not been called. I'm not holding my breath.

CHAPTER

6

Man of the year certainly big enough to wear crown

Man of Year certainly big enough to wear crown

This year, the editors of Time magazine chose the planet Earth as Man of the Year.

I expected better from Time. I don't object if People magazine includes Jessica Rabbit or E.T. as one of the 25 most intriguing personalities of the year.

I think I can appreciate creativity as well as the next man (or planet), but choosing Earth is a little too cutesy for my taste.

I wonder who or what was runner-up? If Earth fits Time's standards as Man of the Year, surely oxygen, pain and electricity weren't far behind. Maybe one of these worthy candidates will be selected next year.

I wonder if the moon will feel cheated for not wining in 1969, the year Neil Armstrong stepped on it. And I hope the sun doesn't turn up the heat this summer because it feels slighted.

Every year I look forward to finding out if I've correctly guess Time's selection. When I'm wrong, I want to feel that I had a chance. But I wouldn't have guessed Earth in a million years.

I wonder how the editors of Time would like it if the Motion Picture Academy picked Orel Hershiser as best movie of the year? Would they think it was clever if George Bush were chosen best country album of the year?

What if your high school social studies teacher assigned a paper on the most important man of the previous year and you turned in a brilliant 250-word essay on why the planet Earth was your choice. Can you imagine what grade you'd get? (Hint: It would begin with F.)

How did these high-priced, supposedly intelligent journalists arrive at their choice? You have to wonder if the selectors were smoking some of the plants that grow on the planet Earth when they made their selection.

There's so little we can count on these days. In a world where men dress up in women's clothing, Russia is our friend and TV evangelists are more sinful than their congregations, I'd at least like to be able to count on Time's Man of the Year being a member of the human race.

Egads! I sound like my parents, listen like them; am I them?

Every so often, an event jars me into realizing I'm not 20 years old anymore. This past week, the 24th anniversary of the John Kennedy assassination and the 20th anniversary of the publication of Rolling Stone could have been the catalyst for such a profound insight.

But what actually triggered the revelation was a late-night compact disc sale at the grand opening of Coconuts. The sale price was small, and the crowd was large. My first hint that this would be a night of introspection was the age of the crowd. Most of them were in their teens, 20s and 30s.

After I made my selection, I stood in line for almost a half-hour with my discs and had the opportunity to listen to two high school kids behind me. They spoke English, but in a jargon totally their own, kind of a cross between Valleyspeak and the dialect of a Carnival shoe salesman.

I was able to understand most of what they said, and it made me feel very old. First of all, one of the kids behind me was buying seven compact discs. With tax, we're talking over $80 here.

Why, when I was your age, kid, I only bought one 45 at a time. I can't imagine being able to afford seven albums at that age. I really can't even afford it now, at my age.

After I got over the shock of teen-age affluence, I listened to them extol the virtues of Jimi Hendrix, The Doors, and The Who. Hey, kid, when you talk about Hendrix, The Doors and The Who, you're talking about my generation, not yours. These kids weren't even born when Jimi Hendrix and Jim Morrison were dying.

I looked down at my discs to satisfy myself that at least my taste had kept pace with the changing times and then it hit me. My musical taste has not only not progressed since the '60s, it has regressed.

I had in my hands a collection of old (circa 1940) standards by Linda Ronstadt, and the sound track from the movie "Radio Days," including such nifty numbers as "Remember Pearl Harbor" and "(There'll Be Blue Birds Over) The White Cliffs of Dover."

I used to pride myself in keeping current with popular music, but when I checked my compact disc collection, I found far more selections from before the '50s than after the '60s.

It's almost as if in protest of the kids of the '80s taking my music of the '60s, I've stolen my parents music of the '40s.

I've known for a while now that when I talk to Jessica I sound like my parents. I've learned to accept that.

It's just very difficult to deal with the fact that I've started to listen like my parents.

'Abbey Road' paves path of instruction

I wrote a column last week about buying some compact discs. Two kids standing behind me spoke in a dialect that was a cross between Valleyspeak and a Carnival shoe salesman. What was more distressing to me was that all of the music they bought was my music of the '60s.

Those two "kids," John Hoyt and Keith Hunter wrote me a letter this week.

"We like to consider ourselves at least semiliterate. We both have English credits in excess of the amount required to graduate high school in the state of Indiana, and we read your column each week."

I never said you were stupid. I just thought you talked funny. But I have to tell you that while most other people may think that passing high school courses proves you're intelligent, I don't. And while I concede that reading my column proves your intelligence beyond any reasonable doubt, most other people wouldn't.

I apologize if your feelings were hurt by my comments about your speech. It's obvious from your letter that you're more than semiliterate. But think how I must feel to discover high school kids are reading my column. I always assumed it was bank presidents, philosophers and orthodontists.

The letter continued to take me to task for saying they weren't entitled to adopt my music for their own. "Come on, Mr. Levco, Hendrix and The Doors were not speaking directly to you and your generation. They were speaking to youth in general. To what are we supposed to listen? (I must note parenthetically here, John and Keith, that I'm extremely impressed by your avoiding the horrible mistake of ending a sentence with a preposition. I'm sure all your English teachers, who gave you passing grades, are proud that you didn't ask, 'What are we supposed to listen to?') Whitney Houston? Madonna? or (gasp!) Wham!?"

Then they moved in for the kill. "We would think that you'd be thrilled to have something in common with young people of today. Like you, we also purchased Abbey Road that night. Give us a chance. We may have more in common than you think."

I give up. No one should have to listen to Madonna. You can have my music. Go ahead and listen to Hendrix and The Doors and Abbey Road, with my blessings.

But I must tell you, it still bothers me that we both bought Abbey Road that night. I'd like to believe the years have graced me with a certain sophistication I didn't have when I was a teenager. Now I find out I'm writing to and listening with a couple of high school kids. No offense.

You say we may have more in common than I think. Of that is what I am afraid.

Running the race of
life and winning

Woody Allen once supposedly said, "Ninety percent of life is just showing up."

When I began writing this article, I researched the quote and apparently Woody actually said, "Eighty percent of success in life is showing up."

No matter. Whether he said 90 or 80, it's a distinction without much of a difference. His point essentially remains the same.

I believe a large percentage of success in life is having the ability to know when to keep quiet and resist the temptation to call a meaningless mistake to someone's attention. It's an ability I have yet to completely master. But I digress (an ability that I have mastered).

Whether it was 90 or 80, Woody could have been talking about me and how I've fared as a runner over the years.

I began running after college, inspired by Jim Fixx's "Complete Book of Running." (For those not familiar with Fixx, he's the running expert who had a heart attack and died while out on a routine run.)

Soon I was entering road races, at the time a relatively new phenomenon.

Phenomenon is not a word anyone ever used to describe me or my running ability. I participated and I finished, but I generally finished in the middle or back of the pack, which was fine with me.

I continued to run over the years, but something unusual happened after I turned 50. Sometimes I would win a trophy in my age group, a third here, a second there and if the race were sparsely attended, even an occasional first.

Had I suddenly become faster? Au contraire. I continued to get slower, but the faster runners in my age group started dropping like flies, some through injuries, some questioned the wisdom of continuing to run or some, like Jim Fixx, actually acquired the ultimate excuse for not running anymore.

Instead of competing against dozens of others in my age group, my competition now numbered in the single digits. As the years have gone by, and I've continued to get slower and older, the frequency of my placing in the top three has increased.

This summer, having advanced to the "I can't believe you're still running, good for you," age group, more commonly known as "Over 65," I have actually finished first two times, with at least one second and third.

I attribute this to hard work, my tenacious competitiveness and the fact there are usually three or fewer in my age group.

I ran in a race earlier this month. There were over 600 runners, 15 of whom were older than I. That put me in the top 3 percent of old people in the race.

Before the race, a guy asked me about applying for Medicare. That's how it is these days at races. I have conversations about retirement benefits and who of our decreasing kind will be the next to literally or figuratively fall by the wayside.

I ran a decent race for me, but I didn't win a trophy this time, primarily because there were more than three others in my age group. But I'm not discouraged.

I know eventually there's another first-place trophy in my future, as long as I continue to run, train hard, do my best – and keep showing up.

Apology from writer over phone call put 20-year bother to rest

I wrote a column for the Indiana Daily at Indiana University in 1969. That spring, I collaborated with a cartoonist, James Larrick, in the IU Primer, on a series of jabs at campus life.

Below is a letter the Daily Student received on the series.

"To the Editor:
Regarding the I.U. Primer
Which doth make my sensibilities simmer.
See the Daily Student columnist
And his sidekick caricaturist,
Who have the sophomoric audacity
To exhibit the exiguity of their sagacity.
Is their intellectual vacuity
To be a perpetual gratuity?
We are tiring of this travestial foist.
By those whose aural posterior is so moist."

It was signed by a Henry B. Walker III.

After I read the letter – and consulted the dictionary – I was impressed. Although the letter was critical of my efforts, it was so well written I decided to call the writer to commend him. We had a brief talk and that was that.

At least, that was that until I received a phone call in April – 20 years later.

"Stan Levco?"

"Yes."

"You probably don't remember me. My name is Henry Walker. I'm calling from Santa Rosa, Calif. I wrote a letter to the editor about something you'd written for the Daily Student in 1969."

"I do remember. Didn't I call you then?"

"Yes. That's why I'm calling you now. To apologize. It's been bothering me for 20 years."

"Just because you wrote a letter to the editor? I thought it was great."

"No, not the letter. The phone call. When you called to thank me, I put someone else on the line. I deceived you. And I'm sorry."

We talked for more than a half-hour that night. Since then we've exchanged letters and calls. This past weekend, Henry returned to Evansville to visit friends.

We met and talked about his letter to the editor, my call and his call to me 20 years later.

He doesn't clearly remember why he put someone up to answering the phone. (Incidentally and coincidentally, that someone is Dave Lamont, a local attorney I have known for more than 10 years. Lamont has no recollection of the incident, but does remember visiting Henry at IU in the spring of 1969.)

Henry's father was a prominent attorney from Evansville who died when Henry was a teenager.

"For a while, after his death, I was virtually a recluse. It took a long time before I was able to deal with it and during that period I did some things I regret, like your phone call."

He's contacted a number of people in recent years to apologize for past actions, but it wasn't until recently that resolving my situation took priority.

"Ten or 15 years ago," he said, "I would have been aware of your phone call and regretted my response, but it wasn't that important to me. I took care of other problems, but the fact that I kept thinking about your phone call made me realize it was something that needed to be acted on."

About a year ago he decided to act, but at first he couldn't even remember the name of the person who wrote the Primer. After a number of false leads, he contacted someone in the archives of the library at IU. He persuaded her to research 20-year-old papers to find my name. He got my phone number from the alumni office.

In this case, his contact was beneficial to both parties.

I'm fascinated by this whole story, partly, I suppose, because it's flattering that someone would be so concerned about something he did to me.

And Henry admits to being "validated" by my reaction.

But the reaction of the contacted person is really secondary for him.

"If someone doesn't respond positively, that's OK. I don't do this as much for them as for me anyway."

"Whenever I resolve one of these matters I feel better about myself. And that's what's important."

They also win immortality
who only stand and walk

They're gonna put me in the movies.
They're gonna make a big star out of me.
The biggest fool that ever hit the big time
And all I gotta do is act naturally.

Every time "Silent Night, Lonely Night," a TV movie starring Shirley Jones and Lloyd Bridges, runs, Isidore Silver, my business law professor at the University of Massachusetts, boards a bus leaving Amherst. He walks up a few steps smoking a pipe. Shirley Jones follows and the bus drives away.

The scene first aired 20 years ago and only lasts a few seconds, but Isidore Silver is preserved for eternity on film.

When I discovered that movie producer John Sayles was at Bush Stadium in Indianapolis filming "Eight Men Out," the story of the 1919 World Series fix, I knew I had to take my stab at film immortality.

Sayles is a friend of John Dempsey, who is a friend of mine. I figured that kind of connection would land me a choice part in the film

Eventually it led to an offer to be part of the crowd scene during the World Series – not exactly the role I'd fantasized about, but a role nonetheless. I toyed with the idea of turning down the part, but since there are no small parts, only small actors, I decided to go for it.

Dempsey agreed to fly out from Boston to join me in the pursuit of celluloid immortality.

Being part of the crowd may be natural for some, but I've always prided myself in being just the opposite. At a concert, if the singer gets to the chorus and exhorts, "OK, everybody sing," if I'm in the crowd, it's a sure thing that everybody won't be singing.

But I wasn't going to forfeit my first movie just because I was being cast against type. So for a week I threw myself into the role.

Luckily the 1987 World Series was on TV. I studied the crowds. I had to throw away some stuff like the wave and hanky-waving, but like any student of acting I was able to find a lot I could use. I carefully watched people standing, walking to their seats, talking, eating and drinking and all sorts of other situations, so I'd be prepared for anything they'd throw at me.

Dempsey and I arrived on the set at 7:30 a.m. First they cut our hair and slicked it back. Then we went to wardrobe where we were outfitted in 1919 suits, shirts, ties and hats.

I soon realized that all my studying would pay off because they put me through a series of crowd variations that might have broken a lesser student. My first role was to stand and talk to Dempsey while he drank a beer, and the crowd acted crowdlike in the background.

I hadn't really practiced standing and talking while a friend drank a beer, although I'd thought about sitting and talking while a friend ate peanuts, but when the camera began rolling, I acted as though I've been doing it all my life.

"J.B. Who are we going to get to watch Paul Newman drink a beer?"

"What about Levco?"

"You mean the guy who watched John Dempsey drink a beer in 'Eight Men Out'?"

"Right. He acted like he's been doing it all his life. Call his agent and see if he's available. And if he's not, at least let's try to get a Stan Levco type."

The next scene they cast me as a man walking down the stairs, while the crowd cheered a play on the field. But no one really explained the part to me.

Just before they began filming I turned to Dempsy, "Why am I walking down the stairs?"

"Because they told you to," he replied.

"No. I mean, in the game. What's my motivation?"

"What difference does it make?"

"It makes a difference believe me. Unless I know why I'm doing it, how can I do it right?"

"OK, then, make believe you're going to the bathroom."

"Number one or number two?"

But before he could answer, I heard a shout of "Action!" and the scene began. I decided not to take any chances, so as I descended the stairs, I concentrated on one and a half. I'm afraid I would have been better off committing myself to one or the other.

"I thought Levco wasn't very believable as the man walking down the stairs, Roger. He had a look on his face like he knew where he was going, but he didn't know what to do once he got there. I give it a thumbs down."

"I'm going to have to disagree, Gene. That certain hint of ambiguity is what made the performance for me. I give it a strong thumbs up."

They saved my best scene for last. I sat behind Christopher Lloyd while he talked to another actor about the fix while I reacted to the action on the field.

During breaks in filming, I was dying to tap Christopher Lloyd on the shoulder and tell him how much I like him in "Taxi," but I decided he'd respect me more if I remained in character.

It was over before I knew it. I had a great time and I'm looking forward to my next movie.

"Whatever happened to Levco?"

"You mean the guy who played in all those crowd scenes 20 years ago in 'Eight Men Out'?"

"Yeah. Every time I see that movie, there he is standing, walking, sitting. Whatever became of him?"

"He got typecast as part of the crowd. Producers were afraid audiences wouldn't accept him in any other role and he never worked a day in the business again."

Bush fans flames of
Beantown bigotry

Most political pundits who sifted through the debris of last Sunday's presidential debate concluded that neither candidate made a major gaffe. I can't agree.

When George Bush accused Michael Dukakis of using "these marvelous Boston words," the audience oohed, indicating they recognized the low blow.

But Bush, not content to leave it alone, reacted to the audience thusly: "People in Boston may not like it, but the rest of the country will know what I'm talking about."

As a former Bostonian and a present resident of the rest of the country, I understand all right. But simply saying I don't like it doesn't tell the whole story.

I feel the same way about Bush's anti-Boston remark that the Duke did about having his patriotism questioned. I resent it. I resent it. (This is how we Bostonians explain that we doubly resent something.)

I didn't realize how the rest of the country felt about Boston until I moved away. But I recognize that non-Bostonians think of the residents of the Hub as know-it-alls.

There's a reason for this. We who are products of Boston grew up with a clarity of thinking that doesn't exist in the rest of the country. Maybe it's the superior seafood, but more likely it's the opportunity to associate with each other.

We try to keep this smugness in check, but sometimes it's impossible. During the second Nixon-Agnew administration, cars (properly pronounced without an "r") around the Bay State sported bumper stickers proclaiming, "Don't blame me. I'm from Massachusetts," a reference to Massachusetts' being the only state to vote against the team that resigned in disgrace.

I know it's things like those bumper stickers that turn people against us. But can we help it if we're always right?

I can accept that Bush tries to exploit Dukakis' philosophy on crime and national defense. And even the flag-waving is just politics.

But this latest fanning of the flames of Beantown bigotry should be beneath even Bush.

Despite our intellectual superiority, we're really not so different from the rest of the country. All most of us want are good jobs at good wages and a chance to see the Red Sox win the World Series in our lifetime.

How much time will $8 million buy Roberts?

According to TV evangelist Oral Roberts, God came to him in March and ordered him to raise $8 million for the Oral Roberts University Medical School. Roberts said, "And he said, 'If you don't do it I'm going to call you home in one year.'"

If this is true I guess it means while you still can't take it with you, you can use it to postpone going for a while. And while money can't buy everything, it can come in very handy if God takes an interest in a medical school.

Since the conversation, Roberts has raised $3.5 million, but with only a few months to go, things are beginning to look bleak. So Roberts has taken to the airwaves to issue his plea for the final $4.5 million so he doesn't get called home in March.

What's God's motive in all this? Why does he want exactly $8 million? Did he get estimates for the construction and go with the lowest bidder? If this fund drive is successful, will God try to get funding for other medical schools? Or will he insist on another more ambitious fund-raiser by Oral Roberts as soon as this one is completed?

I guess if I knew more about their conversation a lot of my questions would be answered. For example, if the money is raised, how much more time on earth will Roberts have? It would be a shame if Roberts raised all the money by March and won the right to live, but then God decided to call him home in April.

Before I raised $8 million or more I'd want to know how much extra time I was buying.

I wonder if there should be some kind of sliding scale. For example, if he raised $7 million, it doesn't seem fair that he should suffer the same fate as if he raised $4 million. I'd hope that anything between $7 million and $8 million would result in maybe a mild flu or a touch of arthritis.

But it's possible, unlike in horseshoes, that "close" doesn't count in raising money to prevent death. I wonder if God would take Visa or MasterCard for the balance if the final total was real close.

I wonder if the $8 million has to be in cash. What if he gets $8 million in pledges by March but the pledges don't come through?

I personally don't have much interest in the Oral Roberts Medical School and I really don't want to contribute. But I worry about what will happen if the final total is $7,999,995. In that instance, how would I ever be able to forgive myself knowing my five bucks would have made the difference between life and death?

It's certainly a dilemma. I could make some small contribution if I had to, but I don't know if I should. I think I'll just wait to see if I hear from God.

If he tells me to contribute, my check will be in the mail.

Did O.J. get bad advice?
I doubt it

O.J. Simpson was back in court this week asking for a new trial, and I'm having a problem with it.

Simpson, who was convicted in a 2007 burglary and kidnapping case, claims his attorney, Yale Galanter, is responsible for the guilty verdicts and the nine- to 33-year prison sentence that O.J.'s serving.

Among other things, O.J. claims his lawyer didn't advise him of a plea offer and failed to persuade him to testify in his own defense. Having O.J. complain about an unfair trial, given his prior experience with the criminal justice system, seems a little like someone winning a million-dollar lottery one day and then complaining about losing a dollar in a scratch-off the next day. But it's not O.J.'s complaint that's causing me a problem. It's my reaction to it that troubles me.

Do I think O.J. received bad advice from his attorney? Highly unlikely.

The advice not to testify and not take a plea deal seemed to have worked pretty well in the murder trial in the case of Nicole Simpson and Ron Goldman. Additionally, Yale Galanter was the defense attorney who gained an acquittal for O.J. in the Florida road-rage case that occurred after the murder trial. Plus, with a name like Yale, you know he has to be really intelligent.

But here's my problem: Even if O.J. got bad advice, I don't care.

Is it possible that O.J. didn't get a fair trial this time? Possible, but hardly probable. But for me, if in actuality he didn't get a fair trial or got bad legal advice, that just makes his present situation more satisfying.

Why is this a problem? Because thinking and expressing these thoughts goes against all my legal training and experience. I don't want to feel guilty (something O.J. clearly was, but didn't feel in his murder trial) about what I'm thinking.

I know everyone's supposed to be entitled to a fair trial no matter who they are or what they did. I really do believe that everyone's entitled to a fair trial. I just don't believe O.J. Simpson's entitled to a fair trial.

It's OK with me if he got a fair trial. I'd even prefer it that way. But if for some reason he didn't get one because of bad attorney advice or because he didn't take a plea deal, then I don't care. (If they fabricated evidence against him, I might have to reconsider.)

Perhaps if a few minor tweaks were made in the criminal justice system, I wouldn't have to feel bad about rooting against O.J.

Two simple O.J. Simpson rules should cure the problem. 1.) If you get away with a double homicide, you can't object to any future verdict against you until you served the time you would have served had you been convicted. In his case, he'd be prevented from complaining for life, since he would have been eligible for a life sentence. 2.) If you have a $33 million verdict against you for murdering two people, as O.J. does, you can't object to another verdict until you pay off the judgment.

I'm not realistically hoping these rules will be implemented in the near future. I'm just hoping that until they are, O.J. will exercise his right to remain silent.

KGB can tell from letters I'm not their man - to say the least

I wrote a column two weeks ago explaining that I felt self-conscious about singing along at rock concerts.

It inspired someone to write a lengthy letter disapproving of my actions.

It struck me that portions of this letter and some others I've received over the years should be shared with our audience of more than one.

Most of the letters I get are critical, unsigned, and make liberal use of exclamation points and capital letters.

"Disgusting" and "ignorant" are two of the most frequently used adjectives.

Last week's letter included the following observations:

"You should be fired from your job," "You are disgusting," and, perhaps the unkindest cut of all, "You are a nerd, to say the least."

While many people who know me would agree that I am disgusting and a nerd, I shudder to think what the letter writer would have called me if he decided to say the most.

Occasionally, a political column will incur a reader's wrath, but it seems that the more trivial the topic, the more personal the reaction.

Basketball in general and Bobby Knight in particular often inspire readers to share their thoughts with me.

One local unnamed coach let me know after I'd written a column about Indiana University's basketball coach that it was "quite obvious that not only do you not know what you're talking about, but you are completely ignorant of coaching and coaching philosophy."

If anybody is more sacrosanct than Bobby, it's Elvis. I wrote what I thought was a rather harmless article on the 10th anniversary of Elvis' death, but apparently some readers didn't think it was so harmless.

Bob Johann, who had the courage to sign his name, observed with admirable brevity, "It must really take a special kind of...to ridicule the dead." Bob included a noun instead of three dots.

Well, Bob, I do like to think of myself as special, but I really didn't intend to ridicule the dead. Besides, I'm sure Elvis wouldn't mind. As a matter of fact, he told me so last week when he phoned me from Michigan.

Another letter to me about Elvis, this one anonymous, said, "Is this the best you can do? Please return to your country. We do not need you here. Do you understand?"

I didn't really understand at the time, but perhaps the letter writer was referring to an article subsequently written by Jack Anderson. The article was sent to me by "a reader."

The article detailed the search for KGB defector, Stanislav Levchenko, who if ever captured by the KGB "will be dragged back to Moscow, marched into a prison courtyard, bound but not blindfolded and shot in the back of the head while his former KGB colleagues witnessed the grim lesson."

"A reader" realized that "people often changed their names and for some reason use only a portion of the former name. Then suddenly your name came to mind and I thought, could you possibly be the man they're looking for?"

I haven't replied to the question for two years, so let me assure you now, comrade, it is definitely not true.

Some letters I get I can really identify with, such as the one I received from David Corn, who discussed a number of topics for a page and a half and ended thusly:

"You may take consolation in this: I haven't the vaguest idea of what I am getting at."

Ron "Pee Wee" Melton wrote: "I read your column every Sunday. I wouldn't miss it for the world, that is unless I go blind. Then I would have someone read it to me."

That's the kind of reaction I hope to get from readers, to say the least.

He won't be spoiled by tennis success

By now I guess just about everybody knows that I won the Mayor's Cup Tennis championship at the Tri-State Racquet Club last Saturday night.

With all the publicity surrounding a big win like this, you might have noticed that I've given no interviews on the subject. That's because with a story this hot I wanted to save all the details for my column.

This, then, is the inside story of how I won the Mayor's Cup.

First of all, since this was a double's tournament, I suppose it's not totally accurate to say "I" won the Mayor's Cup. Some other guy was my doubles partner, and I'd be less than candid if I didn't admit that during the course of our five-match march to victory, the other guy was along side me the entire time.

This was a media-pro tournament. I was the media representative. The other guy was the pro. Many of the spectators thought that the pro, Jeff Braun, a physics professor from the University of Evansville, carried our team to victory. And while an untrained observer may have thought his serves, overheads, and returns were scoring most of our points, any real tennis player knows that hitting the ball is only part of the game – in this case a small part.

While he was putting the ball away, I was doing all the intangibles that turns a good team into a tournament winner. "Way to go, Jeff," I'd say after he'd hit a backhand winner. "Okay, let's get this point," I'd encourage him before a crucial point. And when we'd near the end of a set, I'd say something like, "Let's hang in there. I think we can win this thing."

Not only that, but if a ball was hit between the two of us, I nimbly stepped out of the way to let Jeff get it. My strategy worked like a charm. But I probably couldn't have done it without him.

Now that I'm the champion, I've had a lot of people ask if it's going to change me. Maybe when I was younger it would have been a problem, but I don't think I'll let it affect me at all.

I remember what happened to Mark Spitz after the 1972 Olympics and I'm determined not to let the same thing happen to me. I intend to be very selective in choosing products to endorse.

I've decided not to quit my job so I can play tennis full time. And I'm not going to be in a rush to enter a bunch of other tournaments just to pile up trophies.

I'll just continue to do the things that got me to where I am. I'll play them one game at a time and not let success go to my head.

'Don't be happy, worry' is Levco's latest ditty

Maybe it's the time of year. Or maybe it's the time of man. But I've been worrying a lot lately.

I worry that because the weather's been so warm lately, we'll pay for it with a summer hotter than last year's.

I worry that with a 50 percent pay raise, Congress won't give us 50 percent better service.

I worry that whatever tie I buy the width will be out of style.

I worry that by the time a cure for AIDS is found, there'll be a worse disease.

I worry that, buoyed by this success, Geraldo Rivera will become more extreme – and more popular.

I worry that maybe I'm not getting enough fiber in my diet.

I worry that when Jessica finally gets to Disneyworld, the lines will be too long.

I worry that Michael Dukakis will run for president in 1992.

I worry that someday "L.A. Law" will get canceled.

I worry that some newfangled invention will make my compact discs obsolete.

I worry that Johnny Carson's feelings will be hurt because Pat Sajak is doing so well.

I worry that the drug problem isn't going to get any better.

I worry that inflation will go back to double digits.

I worry that some scientist will say G.D. Ritzy's vanilla is bad for you.

I worry that George Bush won't raise taxes, even if he knows he should.

I worry that the NRA will prevail.

I worry that off-track betting will kill the smaller race tracks.

I worry that the Dan Quayle we've seen so far is the real Dan Quayle.

I worry that by the time a direct highway to Indianapolis is built, I'll be too old to care.

I worry that I don't read enough good literature.

I worry that the Supreme Court will overturn Roe vs. Wade.

I worry that Mary Tyler Moore will keep trying, but she'll never have another hit show.

I worry that I'm really beginning to enjoy all the whining on "Thirtysomething."

I worry that Robin Givens will never be treated fairly by the public.

I worry that the Red Sox will trade Wade Boggs.

I worry that if I ever figure out the answer, I won't remember the question.

CHAPTER

7

From a world far, far away (my world)

From a world far, far away (my world)

Rip Van Winkle slept for 20 years and awoke to a world he couldn't comprehend.

My father, may he rest in peace, was fond of saying in his twilight years, "This is not my world."

I stopped writing a regular column about 20 years ago, announcing my "retirement" on a local Sunday news show in an interview with Lloyd Winnecke. (I wonder whatever happened to him.)

As I contemplate writing a column again on a somewhat regular basis, I can identify with what Rip and my father were thinking.

Things have changed a lot since I last wrote a column. In "Ballad of a Thin Man," when Bob Dylan sang, "Something is happening and you don't know what it is, do you, Mr. Jones?," I felt that I did know what was happening and I was in on it. Not anymore. Now I am Mr. Jones.

The topics I used to write about music, sports, politics are still there, but it's not the same.

Take music, for example.

I used to have more than a passing knowledge of popular music. Today I couldn't name a single song or song lyric of Jay Z's. And what kind of last name is "Z" anyway? And unless everyone else was male, I couldn't pick Lady Antebellum out of a lineup, assuming Lady is a lady and not the group.

I was teaching a class earlier this year at Indiana University and made a clever reference to "Garden Party," one of Ricky Nelson's major hits. When no one reacted, I could have chalked it up to the remark not being funny. Not willing to accept that, I immediately hit upon the cause. "Is anyone here familiar with Ricky Nelson?" Out of a class of 12, not a single hand went up.

What kind of world are we living in when out of 12 otherwise intelligent graduate students, not a single person can identify Ricky Nelson? Not my kind of world, that's for sure.

Sports used to be fodder for satire, but my favorite topic, the inability of the Red Sox to win the World Series, was put to rest in 2004.

Should I write about Josh Hamilton, the game's top home-run hitter, who is covered in tattoos? And what about LeBron James, an otherwise seemingly decent person, who has tattoos over half of his upper body?

I don't get it. Why do they and so many others want to disfigure their bodies like that? Is it possible that they give discounts at restaurants for tattoos and nobody told me? How can I make fun of it when I don't even begin to understand it?

And take politics. Please.

A former favorite technique was to portray a political stance in its extreme to its logical conclusion for comedic effect. But when the extreme becomes reality, there's no place to go for a laugh.

I'm not even sure who I'm writing to anymore. A twenty-something complimented me on a column I wrote a few weeks ago. I was flattered, but rather than graciously accept the compliment, I responded, "I didn't know people your age read the newspaper."

He replied, "I don't. I read it on my iPhone."

He read my column on his iPhone. My column is not written to be read on an iPhone. I write it to be published in newsprint to be read in the paper. Being reprinted in a magazine would be OK, but if I had to write for people reading on iPhones, I'm not sure how, but I'd write it differently. Maybe I'd take a course in Facebook or Twitter, neither of which I know anything about, so that my thoughts were more iPhone friendly.

Writing for iPhone readers is not what I know. And although my universe of knowledge is rapidly shrinking, I need to write about what I know.

I attended the James Taylor concert last week, trying like most others there to recapture the time when I first listened to "Carolina in My Mind" and "Fire and Rain."

It was great. Nothing had changed. Well, maybe his hairline had receded a little and instead of the Ford Center being illuminated by matches, lights from cellphones dotted the darkened arena. Still, it was pretty much my world for about two hours.

I know James Taylor. I know newspapers. And I know Metamucil.

So even though it's no longer my world, I'm still going to write about it.

Sixty-four isn't a Beatles' song lyric any more

"When I get older, losing my hair, many years from now."

I first heard those lyrics in 1967 as a mere lad of 21 on the Sgt. Pepper album, perhaps the most important album in rock music history.

"Will you still need me? Will you still feed me?"

At the time, I didn't give a lot of thought to actually being 64, but I believed that Paul McCartney, who supposedly wrote this song at 16, had painted a pretty accurate picture of what life as a 64-year-old would be like.

"Sunday mornings go for a ride."

My parents, who weren't quite 64 at the time, were already old, and I figured if I should live so long, worrying about who would feed me would be a big concern.

Over the years, I somehow got older and older until…well, you know…as of June 15, I'll actually be as old as the person in the song.

But now that I'm here, 64 is not at all like I imagined.

We baby boomers are not aging quietly. This is not our parents sixty-four. They were so old, but we've convinced ourselves, with hopefully some justification, we're not.

When we sexagenarians get together, we say things to each other like, "I can't believe I'm this old. I don't feel it. I don't look like it. I remember when my parents were this age and they seemed so much older."

I don't think I'm in total denial. The fact is it's not as bad as I feared. After all, 64 may very well be the new 54. I still have some hair and I'm far more likely to go for a run on Sunday morning rather than go for a ride.

But despite my protests, the calendar doesn't lie. I might not be quite the decrepit soul I envisioned in the song, but I realize I'm not going to be able to postpone it indefinitely.

In the immortal words of Sir Paul McCartney, I'm going to have to live with the fact that from now on, I will be "Yours sincerely, wasting away."

I still can't believe it's been 43 years since I first heard that song. I remember it so clearly. It seems more like yesterday.

When words fail you, this advice may suffice

According to a news report, Ronald Reagan says he spends much of his time fighting writer's block.

I've been fighting writer's block since Reagan was hawking for the General Electric Co. on "Death Valley Days," and I daresay I've learned a few things that might be helpful to a beginner.

So, even though he didn't ask me, I have a few suggestions that might help the former president break through:

• Plagiarize – If I had to limit myself to one suggestion, this would be it. If you can't come up with a good idea, find someone who has one and steal it.

Any idea that's worth stealing is worth stealing right. Take it, but put it in your own words.

After you've been in the business for a while, you have the luxury of stealing from yourself. If you like an idea well enough to write about it the first time, it's certainly worth doing at least one more time.

Again, a word to the wise: don't lift it word for word. Ann Landers found this out the hard way.

• Make up stuff – Don't let the facts get in your way. Reality is an obstacle easily overcome by the creative writer.

In your case, it should be particularly easy. If someone challenges your version of a Cabinet meeting, just say, "Oh, I'm sorry. I guess I just don't remember." That strategy worked through eight years of your presidency. There's no reason why it can't serve you well as a writer.

- Complain a lot – If you complain loud and often enough, sometimes others will offer decent suggestions just to get you to shut up.
- Write about your kids – For you, this could be difficult, because you may not know your kids, but it's a great topic when you're stuck.

There are two kinds of readers: Those who want to read about your kids, and the vast majority who couldn't care less.

The beauty of this topic is that those who like to read about it will like everything you write, and those who don't won't bother to read it, and therefore won't realize how badly it was written.

- Use the block to your advantage – the great ones can turn a sow's ear into a silk purse.

Although this advice won't help your writing, it will make you a happier person. If you're blocked, just do things that you like to do.

If Nancy asks you to take out the garbage, just say, "I can't, honey. I've got to write." If you want to ride your horse, just tell Nancy you need to get away to clear your head.

You can justify doing just about anything you want to do on the theory that an unhappy writer is a blocked writer.

I hope this advice is helpful, but if all else fails and you can't think of anything, do what I do. Give advice on how to avoid writer's block.

He took a midlife risk and went the distance

I left Indianapolis Tuesday for Evansville with a quarter of a tank of gas, about what it would take to get me to Terre Haute, Ind. Within a few minutes I'd made a decision: I was going to make it to Terre Haute without stopping, unless I ran out of gas.

I believe if you want to really understand a person, find out how that person fills a gas tank. You'll find out far more about him than if you spent hours discussing the meaning of life.

If I know someone buys gas as soon as the tank is half-empty (or half-full, depending on your degree of optimism), I know that person is early for meetings, files his tax return in February and probably doesn't like "Bloom County."

While I generally fill up at around an eighth of a tank, once I make a commitment to a distance, there's no stopping me.

My quarter of a tank was below an eighth when I was halfway to Terre Haute. I knew this wasn't going to be easy. In order to make it, I was looking at driving the last miles below "E."

I played mind games to stop thinking about the gas gauge by not stopping for gas frequently.

Say I fill up a nearly empty tank once a week and assume each stop takes five minutes. If I filled up the tank when it was half-empty, I would have to stop for gas twice as much.

But I don't claim that I'm playing this game of gasoline chicken to save time. It's deeper than that.

Maybe it's that since reaching middle age, I seem to take fewer and fewer chances. Perhaps my daredevil attitude with my gas tank is my way of compensating for not climbing mountains or parachuting out of planes.

To be sure, there's an element of risk as my tank approaches empty, but the consequences of failing aren't nearly as bad as tripping on a mountain climb or having my parachute fail to open. I have the exhilaration of danger without any grave consequences.

Fifteen miles out of Terre Haute I was on empty. I slowed down a little and coasted on downhills. But I didn't flinch.

I made it to Terre Haute and filled up my tank. I felt like Rocky Balboa in "Rocky I."

But I wonder how much farther I could have gone.

Give a parent an inch, kids, and lose control

Last week, Susie and I went to a program on positive disciplining of children. The program was enlightening, but unfortunately we didn't gain any ground. Unbeknown to us, at exactly the same time Susie and I were attending the meeting, our 5-year-old was attending a meeting of her own.

***

Jessica: I called this meeting because I found out our parents are attending meetings behind our backs to teach them how to regain control of us. I thought a little brainstorming session might help nip this problem in the bud. What technique do you recommend?

Kristin: I like to whine and complain a lot. "You never take me anywhere. We never have anything good to eat. Why do I have to go to bed now?" That kind of thing.

Jessica: What's been your experience when you do that?

Kristin: At first it worked like a charm. I'd say you never take me anywhere and the next thing you know, they'd be taking me out for ice cream or a movie. But lately it doesn't seem to bother them, so I've had to up the ante a little. "You don't love me. You love my sister more than you love me." That usually gets them.

194

Mallory: That doesn't work with my parents. I'll say to my mother, "You don't love me anymore," and she'll just say, "You're right." She must have read a book or something. My dad will still go for it occasionally, though.

Jessica: Parents these days are so much more sophisticated than they used to be. They read books, they watch talk shows.

Mallory: I know what you mean. My 30-year-old walks in the other night and says, "Bedtime is 8 and I mean it." And he sounded like he did, too.

Jessica: What did you do?

Mallory: What else? I negotiated. Finally he agreed to 8:15. I didn't really care about the 15 minutes. It was the principle of the thing. But the intensity in his eyes when he said "I mean it" was scary. I'm afraid next time he'll stick to it.

Jessica: Hey, no problem. Do what I do. Just go to bed at 8, but then get up every 15 minutes for water, to go the bathroom, or whatever. If you do it consistently, they'll learn.

Kristin: I agree. Consistency is important.

Jessica: I know. They just seem to get more frustrated if you're inconsistent. I find it's a lot easier just to never go to bed on time. Keeps their expectations down. That's very important in training a parent. If their expectations are too high, you can never please them.

Mallory: Tell me about it. They're always on my case. But they're so cute when they get mad. I like to bring them right to the brink of losing their temper and then do something funny to break the tension. But I don't know what I'd do without them.

Jessica: I'm the same way. They're a lot of headaches and there are times I think I'll never get them under control, but then I think how much fun they really are.

Kristin: Yeah. Parents. You couldn't get me to take another set for a million dollars, but I wouldn't give away the ones I got for a million dollars either.

Origin of song sung most often

I've got another birthday coming up soon. This seems to happen about the same time every year, but for some reason, more frequently than they used to.

It's likely that sometime during the big day, someone will sing me the "Happy Birthday" song. It's unlikely it'll be sung with the same emotion that Marilyn Monroe sang it to President John F. Kennedy 50 years ago in Madison Square Garden.

If I go to a restaurant and someone tells the servers, I can be sure not to get the real version, which was copyrighted in 1935 and the restaurant would have to pay royalties if their staff sang it.

The song, the most well known and most frequently sung song in the English language, despite the restaurant limitations, was written in 1893 by two Louisville, Ky., schoolteachers, Mildred and Patty Hill.

To be the most successful song ever, there's obviously a certain genius involved in the creative writing process.

I imagine it went something like this:

"Hey, Mildred. Help me out here. I'm trying to write the perfect birthday song, one that will withstand the test of time, but I'm drawing a blank after the first line."

"What's your first line, Patty?"

"Happy birthday to you."

"Happy birthday to you?" Mildred asked.

"Great. That's perfect. Happy birthday to you. Happy birthday to you.

"No, Patty. I wasn't suggesting 'Happy birthday to you' as the second line. I was just repeating what you said."

THE SECOND BEST OF STAN LEVCO

"Doesn't matter. It's exactly what I was looking for. Same number of syllables and it rhymes. And it perfectly reinforces the first line, so there's no mistaking the message. But what do I follow it with?"

"Well, who are you wishing a happy birthday to?"

"I don't know. Let's say, Aunt Gladys."

"Well then, how about, 'Happy birthday, dear Aunt Gladys.'"

"I like that a lot, but what if someone doesn't have an Aunt Gladys?"

"How about just inserting the name of the person whose birthday it is?"

"That's genius. Why didn't I think of that?"

"Don't be too hard on yourself, Patty. You're the one who thought of the first line."

"I guess I did. I think we've got a winner here."

"I don't know. I just can't help feeling something's missing. All great songs need a big finish. Something people will want to sing for hundreds of years."

"How about something like, 'I hope this day of your birth fills you with much happiness."

"That's not bad, but a little wordy. Why not simply, 'Happy birthday to you'? It's simple, yet meaningful. It has symmetry and brings the whole song full circle."

At first Patty was speechless. Then she said, "You're right. How could it possibly end any other way? It's perfect. I can't wait to sing it to Aunt Gladys."

And the rest, as they say, is history.

Keeping up with trends keeps guy tied in knots

Paisley ties are on their way out.

How can I be so sure? Because I finally decided to make the switch to paisley.

I've never had a good relationship with ties. I suspect my problems with ties may be a remnant of my childhood worship of Ted Williams, who refused to wear a tie.

When I grew older, my professions didn't allow for such a statement, so I reluctantly went along with the crowd.

Occasionally I've owned some nice ties, but only if they're gifts. If I buy my own, the results are not pretty. It may have something to do with the fact that I don't mind paying a lot of money for good ice cream or a good seat to the Breeder's Cup, but I hate to pay a lot for a tie.

For over a year now, I've noticed paisleys popping up, but after January it seemed like everyone was wearing them. Somehow the word got out that paisley was in, but no one told me.

I held out for months, hoping they'd go out of style. Last week I decided I could no longer buck the trend, so I went to a local department store to make the transition.

I noticed some paisleys on the rack, but the ones that caught my eye were under a glass counter. This should have been my first clue. Diamonds are supposed to be under glass, maybe even pheasant, but certainly not ties.

"How much is that red paisley?" I asked.

"Fifty," the salesclerk replied.

"Dollars?"

"Yes, $50. It's one of our finest. We're selling a lot of them."

"Actually, I was looking for something not quite so...popular."

"Sir, there are cheaper ones on the rack."

So I went to the rack. It's just as well. Had I bought that $50 tie, it would have been so out of place with the rest of my wardrobe.

That's the trouble with buying a really great tie. People always notice it. By the third time you wear it, they're thinking, "Not that fancy red paisley again. Doesn't that guy ever wear anything else?"

So I bought a couple of forgettable paisleys off the rack and I'll wear them until the day I find out that paisleys are no longer fashionable.

If my past record is any indication, that day won't come for at least another week or two.

Senior status has its privileges

I officially became "The Old Guy" last week.

By most accounts, it was an extremely successful week, but as with most silver linings, there's going to be a cloud somewhere. I suppose an explanation is in order.

First, the good: I tried a week long jury trial in South Bend, and I won.

I know, it's not precisely accurate to say "I" won. Firstly, trials are presumably decided by the evidence. Either the evidence that you present is good enough or it isn't. It's the evidence, not you. More importantly, I hardly did it alone. My co-counsel, the detectives and other witnesses and the jury might point out that they had more than a passing role in the outcome.

Still, if the jury came back with a not guilty, you can be sure I would have lost it, so I'll request a little indulgence in my claim of victory. But as I earlier alluded to, the victory did not come without a downside.

At our table, I was seated near the jury. One time when I whispered something to my co-counsel, I thought I detected a reaction from a couple of the jurors. When I mentioned this during a break, he replied, "I'm not surprised. The jurors can hear what you're whispering."

Before I had a chance to contradict him, the detective chimed in almost apologetically, as if not wanting to offend someone with a disability, "Stan, I've been meaning to tell you this. When you whisper, everyone in the courtroom can hear you. It's almost like you're talking out loud. I'm surprised the judge hasn't said something".

I immediately realized that both they and the jurors couldn't be wrong. The truth was obvious. I had become the person I used to make fun of when I was younger and more recently had sympathy for — "The Old Guy."

You know who I mean. He's the guy who during a movie, thinking he's talking to one person, says things in stage whispers like, "What?" "Speak up, so I can hear you," and "Huh?" that everyone within a 10-foot radius can hear.

I didn't become the old guy overnight. I remember the first time, more than 10 years ago. I got my bill at Hardees, which didn't seem like enough and was told I got the Senior Citizens discount.

"How old do you have to be to qualify?" I asked.

"I dunno, 50 or 55," the cashier replied.

I was both, but even so, at first I thought of rejecting it, but I quickly rationalized, a discount's a discount. Since then, I have embraced the discount like there are a limited number of tomorrows. It's one of the few good things about aging. I now happily accept and even seek it out at every opportunity. Do you know there are some fast-food chains that only charge 49 cents for a senior soft drink? It doesn't get much better than that.

However, I did not accept the realization that I'm unable to control the volume of my whispering with the same attitude as my senior citizen discounts. For the rest of the trial, whenever I thought of whispering, I wrote a note instead. And when the verdict was read, instead of exchanging quiet congratulations, I exercised my right to remain silent until I was outside the courtroom.

The following day, I visited my daughter in Chicago. We took a train downtown. When I got on, I looked for a seat and just when I realized there were none, a young man got up and offered me his.

I said aloud in more than a whisper, "Do I really look that old?"

But no answer was necessary. As soon as the words left my lips, I realized I had unintentionally asked a rhetorical question.

It had been a long week. I was tired. I thanked him, slumped down in the seat and thought about the ride ahead.

Longtime friend lived a life that counted for something

"Time it was and what a time it was
"It was a time of innocence, a time of confidences
"Long ago, it must be, I have a photograph
"Preserve your memories. They're all that's left you."
—*"Bookends Theme"*
by Paul Simon

***

"I'd rather be remembered as someone who challenged you rather than as someone who was nice," Chester told me soon after he'd been diagnosed with AIDS.

Chester died Nov. 26. He was 44.

He was my best friend in college, for me the most important time in life to have a "best friend."

His influence on me during those four years and beyond has probably been greater than anyone, except family members.

He was the one who had the idea to write a satire column in the "U Mass Daily Collegian," which we wrote together for three years under the pen name of Sam Spark.

It wasn't until we were already roommates as teachers in Cleveland that he told me his sexual orientation. Probably had I known about it when we met, it would have made a difference; but when I finally found out, it made about as much difference had I discovered he'd been a closet Yankees fan.

Chester wasn't a very good student in terms of grades or board scores. But, he was a great teacher inside the classroom and out. He had an excellent rapport with his inner-city students, who, on the surface, seemed to have nothing in common with him. Chester's evaluations from the administration downtown were always excellent.

Although Chester achieved success in many areas, including having a book about practical law and numerous poems published, I consider his success as a teacher in Cleveland his single most impressive academic achievement.

Chester was a lawyer by profession, but never really liked practicing law. He quit a few years ago, partly because of his health and partly to concentrate on writing poetry.

It is a bitter irony that the sicker he became, the more success he had getting his poems published in national magazines and books.

He was outrageous, demanding, creative, had an excellent sense of humor, did a great Mick Jagger imitation, and was the life of any party of three or more.

But although his humor was the thing that most people noticed first, it was Chester's intensity that defined him. Chester rarely did anything halfway. He argued passionately for any topic he had an opinion on, which was just about any topic. He wasn't always right, but what made him so appealing to know is that he cared so deeply about so many things.

Chester was in touch with his feelings and helped those close to him get in touch with theirs. He was the best friend I ever had, yet I don't doubt there are dozens of others who would say the same thing about him.

Yet, Chester was not an easy person to be friends with. Any slight, real or imagined, could cause him to turn on someone.

And while Chester was self-analytical, he didn't hesitate to examine others and share freely with them precisely what was wrong with them. It was these qualities that made our relationship, after I moved to Indiana, less than ideal.

We spent a whole lot more time arguing in phone calls, letters and occasional visits than friends should have. But we generally managed to set aside our differences by Dec. 31 every year.

The New Year's Eve tradition began in the early '70s, the first year after I moved to Indiana. I went back to Massachusetts for the holidays and we decided to get together on New Year's Eve.

There were four of us: Chester, Collins, Gaudet and me.

That first year the party was a disaster of such epic proportions that it only made sense to repeat, which we did for about the next 15 years.

One rule was that each of us was responsible for preparing a short bit of entertainment. As the years went by, our skits became more and more elaborate.

Chester invariably gave a satiric news report, which consisted primarily of dumping on those assembled, often breaking the barrier of good taste, but always humorously, particularly when he was making fun of the others.

One of our final New Year's Eves together, about five years ago, was one of the best. That year the others informed me that we would do our skit together – a '60s concert on the Boston Common.

I protested. I thought we'd make fools of ourselves. I was overruled.

Before the concert was over, we attracted a crowd of a few dozen who seemed to enjoy listening to four friends make fools of themselves almost as much as we enjoyed doing it.

That's how I'll remember Chester – playing the chords to "Daydream Believer" in the Boston Common, while Collins tapped out of rhythm on a set of toy drums and Gaudet and I strained to sing in tune.

About a year ago Chester showed me a picture in Newsweek of a crowd in Washington for an AIDS rally. Chester pointed to a blurred face in the front of the crowd that I couldn't recognize, but because of the clothing and the signs near him, Chester could positively identify as his.

He told me how pleased he was that his picture was in the magazine, because the whole point of the march was to be counted. And he was being counted permanently by everyone who saw the photo.

I'll remember Chester for all the good times we had, and even the arguments. And yes, I suppose, I'll remember Chester as someone who challenged me rather than as someone who was nice.

But most of all, I'll remember Chester as someone who counted.

From left to right–Chester, Collins, Gaudet and Levco

I don't go to concerts to hear myself sing

I went on a cruise last week. One of the evening's entertainment was a singer, and it happened again, which it does virtually every time I attend a show of a singer or group.

"Are you ready to have a good time?"

Is this question really necessary? Are there people who attend concerts hoping for a miserable time? And if so, does the singer want you to reply "no" to the question?

Apparently it's not a rhetorical question, because as soon as the chorus or "yes-es" and clapping dies down, the singer follows up with, "I can't hear you. I asked, are you ready to have a good time?"

In the history of entertainment, has the singer ever been able to hear the audience the first time? And I wonder what the singer would do if we either didn't respond or responded "no" to the question. I've never found out because the audience always increased the volume and the singer then does what we paid him to do for a while, until a few songs in.

"I'm going to need a little help on the next one. I'm sure you all know how it goes."

I know how it goes, but I'd prefer that he sing it without my help. And I'm not being modest when I say, even if I did help, I don't think it would improve the performance much.

But if they want my help, shouldn't I have been advised of this before I purchased my ticket? Something like, "Warning: The singer isn't going to be singing every song all the way through. A working knowledge of the lyrics is highly recommended."

And shouldn't I be entitled to a partial refund if I become part of the act – or at least 50 percent off on my next chicken sandwich at Chick-fil-A?

Later on there's an inevitable request for us to clap to help keep the beat. For me, this can be worse than the singing. I can pretend to sing and only those next to me might know I'm not fully participating. I do know how to clap, but any relationship to the beat and my clapping will be purely coincidental.

Then we're back to the singing, only this time it's a competition. "OK, this time I want just the people on my right to sing…Now the people on my left."

Are there actually people in the audience who take pride in being the half that sings louder? Do some audience members leave the auditorium saying, "He was good, but my favorite part was when we sang the left side of the audience under the table."

After the obligatory encore, the singer ends his performance with, "Thank you, you've been a great audience." It's hard to feel too flattered, since I've never not been part of a great audience.

I suppose forced participation is a small price to pay for enjoying a concert, but if establishments can make "no smoking" sections, couldn't they have a "no singing" section?

I know if they did, it might be enough to make me want to clap.

He answered the call and now admits he had hang-ups about money

I hung up on a phone solicitor this week. I'm not proud of it, but here's what happened.

***

"Hello."

"Hello, is Mr. Levco there?"

Already, we're off to a bad start. If the caller doesn't recognize my voice, it's nearly a sure thing that he wants money.

"This is he."

I pride myself in saying "This is he" as opposed to "This is him." It took me a long time to learn it and I say it every time I have the opportunity.

"Mr. Levco, how are you tonight?"

Like he really cares. Why do these people always ask how I am? If I said I was sick or dying, would they discontinue their pitch? (You may be wondering why I didn't write, "As if he really cares." I only pride myself in talking grammatically, not thinking grammatically.)

"Great."

"That's good to hear, Mr. Levco. Did you by any chance read the letter that outlined our proposal for our alumni to contribute 2 percent of their income to the university?"

"Yes. I read it."

I read it and I couldn't believe it. Two percent is about what I'd want to pay for federal taxes. Two percent is what political parties used to charge to keep a political job. But 2 percent to my alma mater? I thought it was about the most ridiculous thing I ever heard.

"Well, what did you think of it?"

"I thought it was about the most ridiculous thing I ever heard."

"I can understand you might think 2 percent is a little high…"

Only by about 1.9 percent.

"But perhaps you'd be interested in becoming a University Fellow. For $10,000, you would be a lifetime fellow and would be entitled to free parking at all the football games."

Who do you think you're talking to, Donald Trump?

"Look, I'm just not interested."

"OK, then how about a five-year, $5,000 plan?"

***

It was at this point that I lost it and hung up on him. I know it wasn't the caller's fault. He was just doing what he was told.

I should have continued to listen to him, if for no other reason than to see how low he'd go.

I'm not proud that I reacted the way I did. And I suppose with the benefit of hindsight, I'd do it differently if I had it to do over again.

But it sure felt good at the time.

Prosecuting kiosks can be hazardous to your health

Most of the time being a prosecutor can be rewarding and enjoyable. Sometimes it can be not so pleasant. I'm not talking theoretical here. I'm not proud to say that I recently had one of those not-so pleasant experiences.

I began an investigation into possible prosecution of video kiosks for distributing materials potentially harmful to minors. With hindsight and a scintilla of foresight this investigation might not have been initiated in the first place. Ultimately, no charges were filed.

Before you consider reporting me to the disciplinary commission, know this: however misguided my judgment may have been, this is not a disciplinary matter. It seemed like the right thing to do at the time. Be assured that the investigation was initiated with equal amounts of good faith and bad judgment. And if bad judgment alone were cause for disbarment, I would have lost my license to practice law long ago.

My first thought upon realizing my mistake was to find someone else to blame, but unlike with most cases I supposedly handle, I actually had done the work myself. Had there been the slightest truth to anyone else being responsible, finding a scapegoat is almost certainly the path I would have chosen.

I knew I needed to accept responsibility, but I wanted to do it in a way that presented my actions in the most favorable light.

Don't get me wrong. I knew I had to tell the truth, but sometimes the truth depends on what the definition of the word "is" is, and once

I made the decision to abandon ship, I needed to do so to minimize the possibility of drowning. Sure, I needed to tell the truth, but not necessarily tell the whole truth and nothing but the truth. I could tell most of the truth and just leave the remainder of the whole truth to my own thoughts.

The first thing I did was to decide to hold a press conference.

Holding a press conference when your goal is to minimize negative publicity may seem counter-intuitive, but I figured if I didn't, the alternative would be worse.

My office is covered by three TV stations, one newspaper and a few radio stations. A press conference had the advantage of limiting the defense of my actions to one explanation. If I didn't limit my explanation to one time, there's no telling how many times I would change my alibi if I were asked to repeat it.

To prepare my statement to the press, I did what all great prosecutors do. I assigned others to do the work.

I asked Doug, my chief deputy, what he thought I ought to say at the press conference. Doug didn't hesitate. "How about this? I want to take full responsibility for my reckless, irresponsible and inappropriate behavior."

"That's a little strong, don't you think?"

"I know I have disappointed my friends, my community and most of all, my wife."

"That's not funny, Doug."

Apparently he didn't agree because he continued, barely being able to control his laughter, "I ask you to respect my family's privacy. They didn't do this. I did."

"Ok, that's enough."

As he was walking out of my office, he couldn't resist adding, "you can always deny using steroids and tell them you're going to go into first amendment rehabilitation."

Since I obviously wasn't getting any help from Doug, I prepared the statement myself.

Everything I said in the news conference was the truth, but fortunately I was able to resist the rest of what I was really thinking.

Good morning. Thank you all for coming here.
(I was hoping no one would show.)

I have decided not to pursue criminal charges against the owners of the kiosks based upon a thorough review of the case law and the facts of the case.
(Although some cynics might say a more thorough review of the case law and the facts of the case before I got in this deep may have been in order.)

Since the law requires that the videos violate community standards, another factor in my decision was that a majority of public sentiment seemed to be against a prosecution.
(Only if you believe 100 % constitutes a majority.)

I received a number of phone calls, e-mails and comments urging me not to continue this investigation.
(How is it possible that 100% of the public can agree on anything?)

I take full responsibility for this decision.
(Trust me. I looked high and low for someone else to blame and if I thought I could get away with it, I probably would have.)

I now consider this matter resolved.
(Please stop calling and sending me e-mails telling me how stupid I am.)

I'm hoping this matter is behind me now. There are plenty of other problems to keep me occupied. And if I never hear the word "kiosk" again, that will be fine with me.

And that's the truth.